Why Self-Love is the Key to True Love

GW00632929

Why Self-Love is the Key to True Love

WHY SELF-LOVE IS THE KEY TO TRUE LOVE...

Dear Elizabeth
Thank you and keep
discovering the power of Love

[signature]

MELODY CHADAMOYO

Why Self-Love is the Key to True Love

Copyright © 2020 by Heart Passion Institute

All rights reserved. No part of this book may be reproduced or transmitted in any form or by any means, electronic or mechanical, including photocopying, recording or by any information storage and retrieval system, without written permission from the author, except for the inclusion of brief quotations in a review. This publication is designed to provide accurate and authoritative information in regard to the subject matter covered. It is sold with the understanding that the publisher is not engaged in rendering legal, accounting or other professional services. If legal advice or other expert assistance is required, the services of a competent professional person should be sought.

Why Self-Love is the Key to True Love is available at special quantity discounts for bulk purchases, for sales promotions, premiums, fundraising, and educational use. For more information, please write to the below address.

Published by: Heart Passion Institute

www.HeartPassionInstitute.com

First Edition, 2020

Cover Art by: Lawson Chad

Published in Ireland

Dedication

This book is dedicated to my late husband Taurai who died in my arms from cancer at the age of 37. I'll never forget our journey and you inspired me to be who I am today.

Epigraph

Kindness in words creates confidence. Kindness in thinking creates profoundness. Kindness in giving creates love.

- Tao Te Ching

What Other's Are Saying

"Melody actually doesn't realize just how good she is, not only is she a fantastic human being with a heart of gold, she has the ability to see things others don't see in a relationship. That can be the difference between happiness and unhappiness. Her story and her openness and honesty for sharing it is not only one of her strengths, but it gives you the confidence of knowing you'll work with someone who has truly seen it all in relationships. I've thoroughly enjoyed seeing Melody's progress as a person and a coach - you're in very safe and loving hands with her. Making the decision to work with Melody will be one of the best things, if not the BEST thing you can do for your relationship"

- **John Mulry, multi #1 bestselling author, strategist and consultant.**

"Melody helped us to re-evaluate our relationship by combining/selecting some of the features within the program with what we had already built, thereby subsequently boosting our

marriage to a level we never anticipated. The program was well delivered, enjoyable, sensitive to our needs and structured to suit us. We would definitely recommend it to anyone either starting off in their relationship or just needing a kick-start to their long relationship so as to get the sparks back in their lives."

- **Alie Hawkins, Dublin**

"Melody's ability to explain the theories used and draw out new ways of thinking in her clients is excellent. Her light-hearted fun approach means everyone will enjoy this course. An excellently designed course. Best of luck with the programme Melody."

- **Maggie**

"My Life Coach Melody is a compassionate, giving woman who is enthusiastic about improving the quality of her client's life. She is a great listener. I really felt heard, and that has been key to my trusting the coaching process. Working with her has shown me that one can actually change her negative thoughts with some simple processes and

feel much better that everything will work out fine and that the Universe has my back. I am not alone."

- **Abir Chammah, Lebanon**

Table of Contents

Why Self-Love is the Key to True Love

.

Acknowledgements

This book would not exist without John Mulry who looked at my work and put it together into chapters that finally became the book. It would've taken maybe 3 more years for the book to be completed. John is a genius at getting books done and for haunting me afterwards to finish. He's so supportive I didn't want to disappoint him so I got to work even when I wasn't feeling the best.

I also want to acknowledge Denise Brett who read and reread the drafts and gave me pointers to nuances that are obvious to a native but not so much to me because English is my second language. She was such a blessing and knowledgeable professionally as well. I loved her honesty and sensitivity to me and to my message.

I also want to acknowledge my sister Neltah who also did a lot of editing for the book. Her honesty and professionalism is admirable despite our relationship. She also had to get it both ways reading the book and listening to me talk about it. It's miracle she didn't throttle me. I also want to thank my brother Lawson for designing the book cover.

My whole family have been supportive and encouraging and I understand that is not always the case when someone gets absorbed by their passion so I want to thank them as well. Last but not least I want to acknowledge, all my clients and people who have opened their hearts to me and told me intimate details of their relationships which helped me learn more and understand more about the science and art of relationships.

Foreword

Love. It's arguably the most sought-after states of being – and ironically, one of the most elusive and misunderstood emotions of all.

Most of the world is seeking an experience of love through external sources: From other people; from circumstances – even from personal accomplishments. This misunderstanding of the real source of love is at the basis of the phenomenon I've been writing about for years, which I call an "outside-in" approach to life, and which will never yield to us the satisfaction we're seeking. Love that we try to garner from others is fleeting at best. At worst, our dependency on it leaves us internally and spiritually bankrupt; lost with no idea of how we got there, or what to do to regain our connection.

Why Self-Love is the Key to True Love speaks about this very phenomenon in language that is both down to earth and easy to understand. It's filled with useful insights and practical exercises that point us back in the direction of the love's true, unlimited source, which is the source that exists within.

Author Melody Chadamoyo boldly shares her extraordinarily moving and personal journey about what it takes to find love, to nurture and sustain it, to heal from the loss of a love, all by learning to love ourselves.

On these pages you will learn exactly how the internal vibration that you are sending out in each and every moment attracts to you the experiences that become the very fabric of your life. And you'll learn that by deliberately adjusting that signal, you can recreate every aspect of your life from the inside out.

The journey toward self-love is one of the most important self-discoveries you will ever embark upon. This book will set you firmly upon that path.

Christy Whitman

New York Times **best-selling author**

Scottsdale, AZ

Why you should read this book?

My name is Melody Chadamoyo. At 19, I met and deeply fell in love with a man called Taurai. Ours was the love books and songs are written about.

We spent most of our courting time living in different cities, but we would write 12 or more-page letters and call each other as much as the communication system in Zimbabwe would allow us.

During those days, we had a functional postal service, thank God! After we got married things started to change between us. I felt like I wasn't first priority to my husband anymore. He would work first and then focus on me.

This didn't bother me as much as the power struggles we were having about money and his need to control how much I spent, add in other minor squabbles and I was ready to walk away.

I wanted a divorce, but I hesitated because I didn't want to separate our daughter from her dad, a dad that she idolized, and I also knew taking our baby away was the cruelest thing I could do to him. I wasn't prepared to hurt him that deeply just because he turned out to be so wrong for me.

I started researching what makes marriages work. I read books like *"Men are from Mars Women are from Venus,"* by John Gray *"Getting the love you want"* by Dr. Harville Hendrix and other books and research papers.

They all pointed out that in order to love I needed to start with me. I started a path to falling in love with my life and me. I joined the gym, started going out with friends, reading and making myself a priority. I also decided NOT to fight with my husband or to take his anger personally.

Instead, I would respond in a kind manner and ask questions for clarity. I later learnt that Taurai took responsibility for my happiness, so he took my unhappiness personally. This is something men do that women don't know.

If you knew that you would ask for what you need more, and you would be happier, and your man would feel good about himself. Slowly but surely, we just started gravitating towards each other. We rediscovered each other. Laughter started again in our home. It took me a while to realize we were back together.

We even started making love again. For the next 6 years we had the most connected beautiful relationship anyone could ever dream of. We practiced loving each other unconditionally understanding we were making a daily choice to be together. I was always a romantic growing up but now I believe in love more than I did before.

The love I believe in is conscious, expansive and demonstrated by the details you continuously add to it daily. The love I believe in is living and needs to be tended and cared for and grown for it to flourish and fulfill your life.
Unfortunately, for me my darling Taurai died in my arms from cancer at 37.

It broke my heart to see my friend, my lover and soul mate go through the trauma of cancer and I couldn't really help him. After a long time of being lost and working very hard to heal my broken heart I decided to use my knowledge and experience to teach other women how to transform their relationships from mediocre and just getting by to awesome like I did.

I wrote this book and I am a practicing Relationship Coach to pay tribute to all the work we did together and the amazing love we shared.

Part 1-

Introduction

Introduction

As a new bride, I thought I knew everything about my husband before we got married. After all, we had dated for 5 years and I really didn't expect any surprises.

Unfortunately, I had no understanding of the fundamental mindset of both the male and female perceptions of marriage and finding myself experiencing very obvious differences in the way we viewed the world woke me up to the gaps that were in my life education. After a great deal of turmoil, I later learnt men and women are fundamentally very different and in order to love and accept my husband I needed to learn more about myself and about men in general.

While it is true men need love, to them it is evidenced in the respect you give to them and not in the nice words you say to them. You can't just say the words and not follow up with action. A man usually demonstrates his love by the practical things he provides for his wife like bringing home the bacon. Women on the other hand want both bacon and the words and if the words are missing, it can create real problems for the man. Discovering these inert differences helped me to appreciate what my husband was giving me and how I could in turn show him love. **I also discovered the real secret to true love – self-love.**

And inside this short book you'll not only go on your own journey of finding self-love, you will also open the pathways to either find your own true love or re-ignite an existing love. I hope you enjoy this as much as I've enjoyed putting it together for you.

Melody Chadamoyo - Heart Passion Institute

www.HeartPassionInstitue.com

Men and Women Are Different

I never really thought about the differences between men and women. I loved my dad and was very close to him, but I never considered how he looked at the world and how it was so different from my mom. I just thought it was because they were different people, but it goes deeper than that.

After I got married, I got onto the activities of making a home. My husband on the other hand started to freak out about whether or not we had enough money. He took sole responsibility for providing for us. I saw this as an insult to me because I wanted to contribute financially too.

We fought about many things, toilet seat left up, who was responsible for what and in most cases; I just wanted him to yield to my will. I thought since I was the woman, he was just supposed to go with what I wanted and how I wanted it. Even though I got my way most of the time, we stopped being as close as we were before. I wanted to show him how competent I was and that I didn't need him to do everything for me. For some reason I had been taught that women are supposed to NOT need men. Instead, women learn to do everything to please the man, except men want you to need them and allow them to do things for you.

They want to contribute and provide for you. I am sure you can see the contradiction in this situation.

Like most people, I wanted a relationship that allowed us to respect each other and to freely express our affection for each other.

However sometimes what I thought was respect and what my husband thought was respect were two different things. When we removed the pressure and other people's definitions and communicated clearly to each other, what we needed, we found more meaning and understanding that created a direction we wanted our relationship to go.

This gave us the freedom to be our true selves in our relationship, so we could easily see when we were out of sync with our goals for example, being defensive when we needed to be more understanding. Coming from Zimbabwe our dating culture is very different from the West. Dating for us was not just for fun but also to learn if the person had the qualities you were looking for. Were they the person you could settle down with one day?

Taurai had the basics and so we moved on to negotiating what was going to be important for us. As we got to know more about each other I discovered that he had all the qualities I was looking for in a man and more. Taurai was the type of man who cleaned up and did laundry before I got there because my purpose in his life was to be with him and not to be his housekeeper.

He used to say things like I centered him and gave him focus and purpose. I had no idea what that meant at the time but now I understand it all.

Discussing our values and having an agreement before we married helped us to recognize when we were not in alignment with them.

Taurai and I understood that like most people, we wanted to have a good relationship, but we had to make a conscious effort to create the ideal partnership that suited both of us.

We had to ensure both of us would do our best to ensure our partnership was built on the most ideal and best elements that would contribute to the strength and longevity of our relationship.

This took honesty, trust, faith and a lot of love with an understating that we deserved to enjoy each other and ourselves. In my case, I remember when we were dating adjusting my approach when I would start getting ready to go meet up with Taurai in Harare City Centre, First Street for our dates and I understood he would not leave home before cleaning up, doing laundry if it was Saturday and cooking lunch for his dad.

Being a guy, he couldn't multi-task which meant everything took longer than it would take me. Instead, of getting there and then getting upset waiting for him, I would arrive 30 minutes to an hour later than we had originally agreed and even though I still had to wait he would get there before I was annoyed, and he appreciated my patience and understanding of his situation.

Finding love requires some initial mental and physical contributions in that you still have to go out there to meet people. You have to make an effort to talk to people. It doesn't matter if you're shy, extrovert or introvert you still need to meet people and open up to them.

When I first met Tau, he wasn't the only guy interested in me; there were a few really nice guys that I had known for longer. I used how I felt when I was with him to choose him. I felt more confident, smarter, relaxed and so happy inside when I was with him than any other man. He didn't seem to be intimidated by my smart answers and strange jokes. I had a lot of respect for him as a person and as a man.

I felt like I could achieve anything and have anything I wanted. I never felt pressured to do anything I didn't want, and

I felt sexy for the first time. I didn't feel that when I kissed him, I was doing a favor for him but rather I was sharing something with someone I wanted to share with. I felt that I could be myself, and it was okay.

As a woman, you should use your instincts to decide if a man is good for you or not. "If in doubt, then don't" is always my motto. I was fortunate to have a wise father who had told me that courtship time is a time to negotiate and agree the fundamentals of your marriage.

Once I had decided that Taurai shared similar values with me. I also observed that I had qualities that were good for him and we began to talk about our future together. We discussed how many children we wanted to have, how we would support and care for our parents and siblings when needed. We even discussed whether or not we would consult a traditional healer if one of us or our children had a medical issue that modern science couldn't resolve. We reached an impasse when I realized he expected me to be a stay at home mom. While I don't have problems with women who take this option, I found this so difficult because that wasn't the vision, I had for myself.

This was a deal breaker for me, and I told him so. I even told him that he might be better off finding someone else because this would never work for me. We stopped our discussions and he went away to think. A few days later, we got together again to continue with our negotiations with an understanding that I would have my own career. At the end of our discussions, we both understood what our values really were. Our partnership resulted in the creation of a magical relationship.

We both understood what we were committing to and our love had created it. I have to say that we didn't sit at a table across from each other talking to each other like lawyers, all our discussions were held during our dates together either hiking, travelling from place to place or just sitting in the botanic garden. Strangely enough sometimes, we woke up in the middle of the night and would ask about something that just came to us in the middle of the night. I know, we were very weird, but it worked for us. We were playful and the aim was never to win or to be right but rather to see if we suited each other fully. Taurai and I did the preparation work and we wanted to ensure that both of us were going to get what we wanted and not compromising on what was important.

In case you're wondering, Taurai's deal breaker for me was that I would never become mushy meaning damsel in distress who needs to be rescued by him all the time. Since I was never like that anyway, this was not an issue for me.

Remember we dated for five years and that time we talked theoretical and practical problems and when we got married, we were very sure of our shared vision for our marriage. Yet I still remember when I was a young bride, I had no idea what I was supposed to do.

Therefore, I started implementing some of the things I heard from friends and society and I found myself terribly unhappy and depressed. Wise women told me marriage was work but nobody could tell me what that entailed.

This was all because I was missing the vital important piece about marriage, a vital piece that brings harmony when acknowledged and used effectively and lacking that almost cost me my marriage.

I didn't know and did not respect the importance of the differences between men and women, the vital piece that brings harmony when acknowledged and used effectively.

Prepare YOURSELF to Find True Love

For some, true love seems to simply pop up and knock them right off their feet into a dream world of wonder and bliss, but for others, finding true love requires quite a bit of conscious effort and even help from people around them including using dating apps like some do these days.

Even when you're playing the "dating game" as some people say, you need to be honest and truthful otherwise you will end up with the person who is not right for you.

Every time we get heartbroken, it leaves scars inside us. Most people don't know that because we learnt to expect scars only from physical injuries. Just think about it for a minute, you've probably heard that if you got a broken leg as a child or a deep cut you can tell if it's going to be cold tomorrow by the reaction you get from this old injury.

That is a memory your body still holds of something that happened in the past, right? How about, scars from emotional traumas we've endured? Have you ever cried over a photograph from the past? All that is evidence of the fact that we carry scars of emotional experiences we have had.

One of the most important ingredients to finding love is to remove emotional scar tissue from past relationship hurts and allow yourself to heal. *"The only way you're going to get 100% participation in a relationship is, if you're not bringing injuries to the table."* Alison Armstrong

Choosing to heal will free your heart and subconscious from the burden of carrying unwanted burdens that stand in your way from opening to real life affirming love experiences.

Most people have built walls to protect themselves because they were hurt in the past and while they are protecting themselves, they can't feel the love even from their own heart. *"The wound is the place where the Light enters you."* Rumi

For me, my scars did not come from having my heart broken by some guy in high school. Some of my scars came from choices my parents made in their relationship that I took personally and blamed myself for. Other scars came from generational choices that brought shame and embarrassment to our family. I had to heal myself from the pain and shame. I also had to wake up to the fact that other people's choices are not mine. I let go of the fear and shame I had been carrying. I also woke up to why some of the words and actions triggered me. Once I healed, I could see when I was reacting from fear instead of love.

True love requires conscious choice and being open to it. Most people don't even realize that they are not open to love because they dislike all men because one man disappointed them. Others believe that love doesn't really exist but just a lie perpetuated by media and Hollywood. Whatever you believe is what you manifest in your life. To manifest is to make real or tangible something that is imagined in your head.

When you go around finding fault or blame in every man you meet instead of healing yourself, so you can open yourself to finding the love inside your heart, you miss out on having great life experiences. Just because the relationship didn't lead to long term commitment or marriage doesn't mean it was a failure. You learn a lot about yourself and grow in every relationship.

You use excuses of your past experiences to stop yourself from being hurt again. Speaking as a person who has loved deeply and intensely and then having my husband die, I know for a fact that love doesn't die. In fact, having love inside means you should grow it, tend to it, experience it, and share it in many different ways because it is what gives life meaning. I am more myself because I love, and I am loved.

As you go on your path to seek true love you have to understand, there are no quick fixes and that if you are seeking true love, consider exploring all avenues present, as this will definitely help to lessen the disappointing possibilities as they arise. Remember seeking does not mean finding immediately. You have to decide if what you find is right for you and not just close enough. Many broken hearts happen because women choose men who tick most of the boxes or close enough but are not quite right. Sometimes when a woman likes a man, she is eager to meet his every need in return for very little attention. I find it amazing how much some people will give up just to have someone in their lives.

You need to do your due diligence and if you rush and commit to Mr. Almost Right, don't complain when you start feeling like something is missing. Have patience and faith that you will find what you're seeking. Finding Mr. Almost Right is evidence that there are people who have those qualities and should be encouraging to you.

The Universe is very generous, it will give you what you want but you have to believe that you deserve it and open up to receive it.

The following are some of the best tips to finding true love while minimizing disappointment:

Most experts say you need to find and understand your true self first, before attempting to find comfort in love from an outside source. If you could learn to be at peace and feel happiness without the need for outside affirmation, you would be starting from a good place.

You can't give what you don't have. Learn to love yourself. Do the things you enjoy. Fill yourself up with kindness, love and joy and then share it with others. I teach this in all my programs because everything starts with you.

Grow the skill of being comfortable with yourself and being able to spend time alone and enjoying your own company and all things that should be acceptable to you as an individual before embarking on the quest to include others into the equation.

To find true love, you should first be able to love yourself for what and who you are. This means accepting both your flaws and your strengths. This is shown in the way you treat yourself and how you go about your daily life.

Once you know how to treat yourself, others will learn from you how to treat you. This is so important in order to create good boundaries in any of your relationships.

Therefore, if you are totally comfortable with your own personality and everything that is included within your personality, only then will you be able to seek and find love outside these perimeters.

We'll be covering this part in depth in Part 2 of this book – where we will be diving deep into self-love.

Patience is another very important element to exercise when it comes to finding and keeping true love. You will miss opportunities for deeper connection if you're not able to exercise patience and caution when seeking out relationships with the intention of establishing a strong and loving relationship. Most people have baggage and scars from their previous relationships so exercising patience will help you to understand when a person is operating from fear or from ignorance.

Clear communication is key, and it is important to clarify situations at all times, even if it's to say, "I'm confused." For some reason, I was always very clear about the type of man I wanted to marry but my friends in boarding school kept on telling me such a man didn't exist.

Strange things happened (that are beyond the scope of this book) that transpired for me to meet the man I eventually married.

I was 19 and boys were asking me out on a regular basis but for some reason they didn't appeal to me. Many people couldn't understand why I chose a man who had albinism instead of them or anyone else.

I saw much more than just his skin, I saw light and love, intelligence, fun and oh, how I really wanted to bask in his light. Every day he surprised me with his awesomeness. I loved how I felt when I was with him. If I had followed society's definition of ideal, I would've missed out on an amazing love experience that still amazes me to this day.

Getting caught up in life

Often people are either too caught up in their own life pursuits or are simply too clueless to recognize the beginnings of true love in existing relationships.

Sometimes people miss out on the right person because they get caught up on the idea of type or other society hang-ups that were devised to separate people instead of fostering love. Vishen Lakhiani talks about Brules (Bullshit rules) that society created to tell you that you should marry a person from your race, religion, height, hair color, tall, dark and handsome or whatever.

However, those who have been lucky enough or taken the time to find true love explain that there are certain indications that can show you that you have found the one. You will know that you have found true love when you start to feel the following:

You can't help yourself and you want to be with the other person all the time because being with them gives you a sense of peace. You find yourself suddenly unwilling to go on dates with new people and would rather spend time with a particular person, this is the first indication to the possibility of a true love relationship prospect developing.

You have now stopped searching and feel you can build something with the person you have found.

When you want to be exclusively available to one person and feel totally comfortable about such a choice it is definitely a strong indication to go by.

Another good indication to you would be that you are no longer interested in keeping in touch with all the people listed in the famously termed "black book".

Making the choice to no longer need the company of those listed in the black book in favor of one particular person, would indeed show a clear leaning towards feelings that are deeper and perhaps ones that will eventually evolve towards true love. If you're willing to try new things that would otherwise not be from your normal choice of activities, this is also an indication that this particular relationship could have the potential of becoming something worthwhile.

Ladies when you find a man who is willing to go out of his way to do something for you then it means he cares deeply about you. Tread carefully because you might unintentionally break someone's heart if you're not interested in them. You have to gently break ties as soon as possible so you don't give the wrong message or false hope.

I knew I loved Taurai when I discovered I was willing to wait for him for 2 hours or more just to see him when he was late for a date. I don't particularly like walking, but I would go hiking with him for hours. I developed such great patience for him and understood his weaknesses and strengths. I was willing to consider other perspectives as long as it meant we stayed together.

It is good practice to take a step back and review all the things you're doing within this new relationship in order to accommodate the other person. This will show the individual just how much value you're giving the other person's company and companionship. While you're taking stock of what you're willing to do to be in the relationship, you also need to examine what he is sacrificing to be with you.

If the idea or prospect, of spending time with this person exploring the relationship brings on excitement and anticipation, it is also another good indication of the possibility of true love forming.

Wanting to be in the other person's company as much as possible is definitely the beginnings of something that is budding and about to bloom.

Taurai and I took every opportunity to be together that we both would drive all night to get to each other. We felt so much peace with each other that sometimes we were driven by a hunger and desperation to be together both of us couldn't understand.

Why Self-Love is the Key to True Love

Part 2 –

Self-Love

What is Self-Love?

In this part of the book we will be diving deep into the topic of Self Love and how you can find it and use it to have the confidence and clarity about finding your own true love.

Self-love is perhaps one of the most fundamental yet misunderstood concepts in the world right now. Some dismiss it as a new age ideology that cannot be applied in practical terms. However, nothing could be further from the truth. This book will show you practical steps with regard to developing self-love. It will also explain what self-love is and outline the history of the trait and how self-love is the core foundation of all spiritual teachings.

Self-love is the ultimate way to boost your self-esteem and become a fully healed and integrated human being. People often come at the idea backwards.

They look at attributes other people have such as the way that a confident person walks or they observe their traits. Fundamentally, all radical change begins from within. You then start to really value yourself as a powerful creator of your own reality and deserving of love and respect from everybody.

Self-love is the opposite of selfish. You are unable to love another person unconditionally unless you love yourself first. Self-love is not about engaging in destructive patterns of behavior and turning a blind eye. It has nothing to do with arrogance or narcissism and everything to do with becoming a whole and integrated individual.

When you are able to exercise self-love, your life will become so much easier. This is because you will not sabotage yourself as much; which is what everybody does with their beliefs about unworthiness.

You will also have much more stability in your life as you will no longer depend on others for fulfillment. Your emotions and reactions will not be volatile, and you will actually not personalise a lot of stuff that goes on in the world.

Love is the ultimate building block of the entire Universe. Humans are born into the arms of loving parents and they die ideally in the arms of their loved ones. They live and die by love alone. In the words of Gautama Buddha:

"In the end, only three things matter: how much you loved, how gently you lived, and how gracefully you let go of things not meant for you"

Your ability to love yourself and others is all that really matters. How to get there is another matter entirely. For this, you have to find out who you are and love yourself unconditionally.

Finding the Self

Finding the self is a mystical concept that has been around since ancient times. The 'self' has been described by many names, such as the soul, the over soul, the atman, the monad, the "I AM" presence, the Christos, the illumined one, and so on. Labels aside, the self can be described as who you truly are without any of the social behaviors and attitudes that you have downloaded since birth. It can be 'found' by shedding illusion and peeling away the layers of programming, which can also be called the ego.

The entire process of childhood and socialization is essentially learning how to forget who we really are. Our peers and parents scold us when we do something that does not conform to their viewpoint. As such, we learn how to behave in a prescribed way so that we can be accepted.

Being part of a group, family or tribe is the single most important social norm. This dates back to a time where non-conformity would have gotten us thrown out of the tribe - likely to starve or freeze to death. Pleasing others is ingrained deep within us, but it is also very harmful in terms of spiritual evolution.

So, after we are born, we experience traumas that make us forget who we are. We are programmed from what foods to eat, what language to speak, how we view others and how we participate and contribute to society. Examining and letting go of beliefs that don't serve you is necessary in order to connect with yourself.

You may even go into what Freud calls "the imperatives of the superego where you give yourself pressure by saying, I should do this, or I should do that."

For example, you might see yourself as the only person capable of doing a good job so you cause yourself stress by taking on more than you should. You micromanage your colleagues and nitpick on their work because you believe that only you are capable of doing exceptional work.

And, we then have to go through the process of

forgetting everything we learnt in school and through wider society to find our true selves. Sadly, reconnecting is anything but easy in the modern age. Technology ensures that information is everywhere so we will look everywhere but inside - where the self-resides.

How to Find the "Self"

There is a defined path to find the self "quickly", though the process cannot be described as quick.

Many people are swift to dismiss Eastern modalities as outdated, unusual, and unworkable. But, the fact of the matter is that in terms of finding the self, Vedic philosophy occupies a distinct position of respect.

To proceed with finding self, you will need:

- A silent and serene location

- The ability to meditate on the heart chakra

- The ability to severely restrict diet

- The ability to leave behind all technology and distractions

In many ways, it is simple and straightforward. Get to a silent location and meditate on loving the self. Restrict your diet so you are not eating any meat, processed food, caffeine, or alcohol.

Avoid technology and eliminate all mental, physical, and emotional distractions. Though this can be difficult to do, the results will be immense. It is the ideal healing modality. 3 - 7 days is enough for significant changes to occur with the above protocol. It can be repeated as often as necessary and while you won't succeed the first or even the tenth time, it is enough to fully rejuvenate you from the stresses of modern living in a big way.

Ironically, the quickest way to find the self is to do absolutely nothing at all. Your body, mind, and soul will heal if you just stop eating, thinking, and reading garbage material all the time. You will be in a perfect state of health if you stop doing things that put you in a depressed mood and environment. The grand irony of it all is that people feel the need to 'do something' to fix an illusory problem. This leads to fad diets, liposuction, unhappy relationships, and unaffordable mortgages, among other things.

Vedic philosophy has by no means a stranglehold on silent retreats and fasting. However, it really cuts to the heart of the matter with its emphasis on these things and its constant focus on finding the self.

There are hundreds of other esoteric modalities such as crystal bowls, visualization, spinning, manifestation, lucid dreaming, chakra work and many more.

While they might bring many benefits and even some paranormal effects, they do not cut to the core of finding the self. This involves letting go of everything you have learned to step into new dimensions.

The pinnacle of self-esteem ultimately culminates in self-realization; a state of being that is talked about in practically every piece of spiritual literature of note. This state goes beyond the typical human experience to full-bodied bliss and understanding. However, self-realized people are still flesh and blood, live to tell their experiences, have written books, and can be found by those who actively search for them.

Other Methods to Help Find the Self

There are more ways to find who you really are. It is like peeling an onion where only the true self is left. A good place to start is to review all of what has happened to you in this lifetime and the major events.

The point is not to wallow in them or take pride in achievements. Just draw a linear map of the major events that happened, what their effect on you was, and try to see the bigger picture. This will help to build a degree of objectivity.

In terms of finding self, you do not want to be dependent in any way. So, look at all the ways you are emotionally, mentally, physically, or financially dependent on other people and things. Become as self-sufficient as possible while not isolating yourself. Always looking back is depending on the past, which does not serve you now. Looking fearfully in the future will also not serve you now. Finding self is an individual process. Nobody has ever self- realized themselves together. The Universe doesn't work that way. It is a personal journey that you take alone. This could entail an elimination of cigarettes or certain unhealthy foods or finding a new job where you work for yourself. It will be different for everybody.

Groupthink is the antithesis of individual empowerment. Because even in groups, solutions only come from one individual with one spark of inspiration.

There is no way to share creativity or ingenuity because it comes from within. This means that when you are finding the self, the practices that you use and the philosophy that you adopt will be yours alone.

If you simply copy what others are doing, then you are

already disempowered, and will never find the self. Without making decisions of your own volition, you are not giving yourself any power.

Self-Love and the Shadow

Self-Love is a lifelong practice that has to be fully attended to in order to bring about its full effects. In the current era, "the law of attraction", is very popular and comes with a myriad of benefits.

It refers to the fundamental nature of the universe; that we have but one thing in our power, which is our attention. This means whatever we turn our attention to, we attract towards us.

Some authors have indicated that attention is love and that whatever we love or put our attention on simply grows bigger.

So, we must be discerning in where we place our attention. It is worth noting that the two biggest fields in spiritual psychology - shadow work and positive psychology - are adamant that people should only focus on bettering themselves and will, therefore, better the world consequently.

Shadow work is a critical piece of the puzzle in terms or self- realization and empowerment. It has taken centre stage from the law of attraction. According to Carl Jung, enlightenment can only happen through shadow work:

"One does not become enlightened by imagining figures of light, but by making the darkness conscious"

It is also worth mentioning that when the Law of Attraction is studied in detail over the course of all the videos and texts, the shadow self is comprehensively dealt with.

Over time, the person will attract instances where the dark side is healed without making it the main priority. This could be in the dream state or in physical reality. You start to separate the events that happen in your life from your identity.

All About the Shadow

Shadow work was first brought to the mainstream attention through the work of the eminent psychologist and behavioral therapist Carl Jung. He examined the shadow side of the human being primarily through the dream states as well as symbols.

He also discovered something called the collective unconscious, which all humans share. However, this is not relevant to the personal purpose of finding the self. You do not need to investigate the theory to complete the tasks. The theory always comes second to practical experience.

As per Jung, everybody has a shadow self which needs to be integrated. The less that the person integrates the shadow and expresses it openly, the blacker and denser it will be. Additionally, the shadow will often project its own failings onto other people.

This phenomenon is often demonstrated in Law of Attraction teachings, where we notice things in others that we hate about ourselves. In other words, our weaknesses and irritations can be the best tools for introspection.

According to some authors, the shadow self is actually the seat of creativity and has many positive aspects. It is just that certain attributes are now viewed upon favorably by our current society.

Alternatively, the individual might have just had a certain experience that forced him or her to repress certain emotions and behaviors. Regardless, everybody has a shadow side that needs to be tended to.

For some, it is more obvious than others and you can use other people as a mirror to understand your own shadow.

It will be oblivious to you but clear to those who know you. For Carl Jung, the shadow self was a monster both individually and collectively:

"It is a frightening thought that man also has a shadow side to him, consisting not just of little weaknesses- and foibles, but of a positively demonic dynamism. The individual seldom knows anything of this; to him, as an individual, it is incredible that he should ever in any circumstances go beyond himself. But let these harmless creatures form a mass, and there emerges a raging monster."

The Dark Side of Self Love

The fact is that human beings learn far more from their pain than they do from their triumphs. We have far more to learn from our faults than our strengths. Mirroring is an excellent technique that everybody would benefit from and can greatly assist in self-love. Everybody can be used as a mirror for our own development.

When we detest somebody else, it is a flaw in our own perception. What you see in others reflects to you what you have within yourself but do not want to deal with.

As a result, when somebody bothers you, it is easier to project your own failings onto them and criticize. As per German author Hermann Hesse:

"If you hate a person, you hate something in him that is part of yourself. What isn't part of ourselves doesn't disturb us"

Again, this is reflected in the law of attraction. When we judge or condemn others, we are criticizing things we are unable to deal with within ourselves.

The Christian bible also reflects these teachings: *"You,*

therefore, have no excuse, you who pass judgment on someone else, for at whatever point you judge another, you are condemning yourself, because you who pass judgment do the same things" (Romans 2:1)

"Do not judge, or you too shall be judged" (Matthew 7:1)

The Ego

The ego is the part of personality that we call self or I. It is the part of you that remembers, plans and evaluates in response to the physical and social world.

The ego as part of you will work to protect you by evaluating whether or not you will be safe before taking a particular action according to what might have happened in the past. For example, maybe you were called out by the teacher when you were in First class and failed to spell a word and other kids laughed at you.

The ego is the one that tells you that you have a fear of public speaking in order to protect you from the embarrassment you felt when you were still a child. Most of the shoulds and have tos are because the ego is driving the action. You do things because you think you should so that you can feel valuable. I used to insist that my husband do things my way because I felt that if he cleaned the kitchen counters his way then that diminished my ability of cleaning. As a result, my insistence to do everything myself made me feel overwhelmed, unappreciated and exhausted. When I learnt to quiet my ego and accept help, my life became easier and more fun.

Building Self-Love

If you want to build up self-love, the first thing that you have to do is purification. The reality is that most people have picked up a lot of wild and irrational beliefs, values and attitudes that are not real. They cause a lot of damage. There are also a lot of physical toxins in the body from an unclean environment.

Purification

You need to purify across all levels in order to love yourself fully. Purification might sound like a drastic step, but it is certainly worth it so you can see yourself with more clarity. Purification generally involves:

- Fasting or dietary restriction.

- Information restriction.

- A natural environment.

- Meditation.

- Prayer.

- Yoga and/or exercise.

- Reading of uplifting material.

- Silence.

- Sleeping

You can do a combination of the above for as long as you want. 3 days is the minimum and 3 weeks will have incredible benefits.

Taking the time to learn a new skill and embed it in your mind is worth doing. These techniques are ancient and despite all of the new age positivity strategies, they work the best.

Nothing will have the same impact as doing the above in tandem with one another. They work individually, but the effects are magnified when combined. It is only when you get away from society (i.e. "real" life) and do these practices that you can clearly see just how dysfunctional society really is and how dysfunctional your own beliefs and thoughts are about yourself and about society.

Day to Day Exercises

Not everybody has time for an intense purification exercise. They can only really be done once every 3 months or so. Due to this, people need less intense modalities so they can build self-love steadily and consistently over time.

The first step is in relation to freeing up your time and energy. Most people have heavy stress either from energy vampires or from work and relationships. The best scenario, if possible, is to simply exit a toxic relationship or environment.

Many people are afraid of leaving a job they hate and pretend that they have to stay there to pay the bills. However, nothing is worth having your energy drained and living like a zombie with no purpose or intention.

What happens is that you are pretending to be someone

you are not, which is the polar opposite of authenticity. I once stayed in a toxic environment for a job. I justified all the angst and suffering this brought to my health until my body just gave up. One day my lung collapsed, and I nearly died. I had to get real after that and left this environment. I should point out that I made a decision to leave and within a few months, I had found another job whereas before I had told myself that I had no choice.

You need to listen to your body because trauma is written on your body. Our bodies always tell the truth no matter what our words say. If you ignore the message one day, your body will just collapse. Listening and taking care of your body is a self-love practice.

There are many self-love exercises you can do, but here are 5 of the most effective:

- The waking and sleeping hours are a prime time to master your thoughts and emotions. In the place between sleeping and waking, turn your thoughts as positive as possible.

These states are more powerful and set the tone for the rest of the day or night.

- Keeping a gratitude journal is perfect for appreciating the good that come daily into your life. The fact of the matter is that human appreciation is arbitrary and irrational.

We can work towards a goal for 5 years and appreciate its completion for a week. We need to reframe our gratitude and appreciation so we can be joyful for everything, not just the big goals. We need to be grateful for every step we take towards achieving our goal. This will put us in the right frame to succeed and speed up our progress.

- Put yourself first with vacations, massages, extreme sports, concerts, whatever it is that you want to do. You deserve supreme enjoyment, and it is what you are here for. Sadly, most people think that life is supposed to be a painful chore and create stress for themselves. Do not do this to yourself!

- Stop interfering with others at all costs. There is a kind of virus going around where people are trying to make the world a better place and love pointing out the flaws in the world. This is in spite of the fact that times have never been better, by a gigantic margin. If you do not focus on your own self-development, you will never develop and you will find others interfering in your life in a similar fashion.

- Meditating on love or focusing on the heart chakra is a chief recommendation among ancient spiritual scriptures. The heart chakra is a doorway to the higher self/oversoul if you put your energy there for extended periods. Your heart will open and allow magical experiences to enter your life.

Feel Good at All Times

One of the most important and overlooked parts of being able to find the self is being unashamed about feeling good. This entails doing activities that feel good to you as much as possible.

There is a tendency to believe that you must suffer much

to 'achieve' happiness. It is more the case that unhappiness has to be 'unlearned' from past conditioning. There is no reward for suffering.

There is nothing wrong with feeling good, and there's nobody who is not worthy of self-love, respect, and appreciation. There is actually no reason you have to work for 4 years in university to start out on the corporate ladder and work your way up unless you want to.

This is actually quite silly, given that you can get certified from a distance and set up an online business for a fraction of both the cost and time. Yet people still flock to universities paying tens of thousands of euro or dollars to wait 4 years until they can make an income if they get a job after they acquire the graduate degree. I am not saying don't go to university if that's what you want because I have a Masters' degree but do it only if it is what you want not what others are making you do.

In any case, you don't have to accept any limitation that society places upon you. If you want to master self-love, then you have to love yourself and treat yourself with respect. This entails saying no to toxic relationships, setting boundaries, thinking positive thoughts, journaling, getting exercise, getting massages, going for luxurious hot showers, taking regular vacations or whatever floats your boat. Your only responsibility is to yourself and to make sure you are as happy as you can be.

Signs when you are not loving yourself

Sometimes you might have an illusion that you love yourself when in fact your actions reflect the opposite. Most people have not even thought about whether they love themselves and how that feels like. Here is a list of some of the things you might do that will show you that you're not loving yourself:

- Allowing people to mistreat you like controlling you, beating you, bullying and any other form of mistreatment you can think of. There was a time when I allowed my former boss to mistreat me. Once I woke up to who I was, I had the strength to challenge it and make him stop. This happened because I was not self-aware at the time. Who are you allowing to mistreat you and why?

- Doing drugs is another way of showing lack of love for your well-being. You know the hurt and pain being under the influence is to you and everyone who loves you. I am not judging you, but I am attempting to show you what is happening inside you. Is it time to wake up to who you are?

- Self-sabotage is when you meet a great guy/girl, fall in love and then you do everything you can to destroy that relationship. You might cheat or lie and do things that you know will drive the other person away. Sometimes you pretend to be someone you're not in order to attract a person for the wrong reasons like maybe they have money or a high social position or something. What are you doing that is not serving you?

- You might also not rise to your potential, procrastinate all the time, sexually promiscuous, blame others or not take responsibility, refuse to receive, give more than you're able to, serve others out of duty or love at your own expense, never have fun, do things for others in order to get attention or love. Never giving yourself treats or luxuries. What are you not allowing yourself to receive?

If you find some of the things you do on the list, this is not a time to judge yourself. This is the time to find healing for that which has made you reject your true self. It is a time to evaluate and take charge of your life.

Reaffirm your commitment to yourself and start on the path back to loving yourself. It is only when you're whole that you're able to share yourself with others.

"We can only love the world to the extent that we love ourselves. Loving the world while not loving yourself, from a certain

point of view, is hypocrisy. You will eventually burn out if you try to

extract yourself from something you lack." - Ilchi Lee

Alternative Self-Love Strategies

There are actually wide varieties of self-love strategies. What's important to understand is that it is not really an additive process. You need to shed the skin or beliefs, values and attitudes that you adopted to protect yourself in this life. Being in a relaxed state of mind helps you to do this. Anything that gives you another perspective and leads you away from erroneous beliefs can be termed a self-love strategy.

Books on Self-Love

Of course, there are no shortages of spiritual teachers who can share a lot of wisdom when it comes to self-love. Krishnamurti, Osho, Alan Watts, Sadhguru, Tolle, the Dalai Lama, the list goes on. All of them offer a different perspective with regard to how to achieve self-realization. But only a select few identify love as the true source and deal with it directly.

One of the modern teachers that does, is called Don

Miguel Ruiz, who is a Shaman and proponent of Toltec wisdom. His books have been international bestsellers and include The Four Agreements, the Fifth Agreement, The Voice of Knowledge, and The Mastery of Love. Another powerful speaker on self-love is Marianne Williamson. Her first book, A Return to Love had a major impact on many others and me.

There are many books to choose from in terms of reading. It is important not to be critical or judgmental of any book you read. If it's not for you, just put it down and select another that is more appropriate.

Don't feel the need to write a 1000-word review about how bad it was. The negativity will just bounce back to you. In any case, love is to be expressed and developed, and there is only so much that you can learn from books alone, regardless of how well the material happens to be. Practice beats theory all the time.

Quickest Paths to Self-Love

To love yourself, you must look at yourself clearly. Doing this is not as easy as you might think. Most people have an idea of themselves that they associate with their jobs and accomplishments. These ideas have nothing to do with reality, whether they are positive or negative.

Mirror gazing is a good way to really look at yourself. The eyes are said to be the windows to the soul, and you might find looking directly into your own eyes to be very uncomfortable. Try gazing at your own eyes for a few minutes every morning. You can also do this with a partner to increase love for each other. Remember, the main reason that you do not love yourself is that you cannot really see yourself due to a lack of perception. Any kind of modality that clears your mind and your perceptual lens assists you in self-love and compassion of others.

Compassion itself is not really a 'path' or means to self-love. What happens is that when you become more self-loving, you become more compassionate towards others. When you give yourself something like respect, understanding, acceptance and compassion, you start to see others as deserving of those attributes as well.

In terms of the shadow, what you see in others you detest, as it is alive within you. But when the shadow has been integrated, you are more compassionate to those who suffer from the issues that you have integrated. You recognize them more clearly because you used to have them, and your compassion is far greater because of the integration.

Discipline and focus can be a means to self-love. This entails moving away from automatic behaviors which are not serving you. But it can be very tricky to get the balance right between being dogmatic and disciplined. Some people can become extremists and are unable to enjoy the simple joys. Yet for the vast majority, the difficulty lies in a lack of discipline and constant indulgences.

In any case, advertising, social media, processed foods, alcohol, and cigarettes should be minimized as much as possible. If you really love your body, you will make the effort and treat it right with exercise and a reasonable diet.

Nothing really beats meditating on love and generating it as raw emotion. This is a professional practice for people who dedicate their time to attain a mastery of love. It is the most direct approach of really feeling the energy of love and directing it at an object and towards yourself.

Organization and Cleanliness

While this is secondary, try to clean up the outside environment as much as possible. This means that your room and desk is as clean as possible. You might also want to throw out some of your old stuff or do a garage sale. This is very therapeutic and should serve to clean the mind. You need to put yourself in a safe, clean, and organized environment.

You also want to rid yourself of any toxic relationships that you have. Toxic relationships in the home or workplace will sap your energy like nothing else. While you are angry, fearful, or ashamed, you are blocking the energy of love. Understand that it is not possible to feel a positive and negative emotion at the same time. When you are feeling fearful, you are not loving. If you can manage to generate loving emotions in the midst of a depression or crisis, then it is possible to drag yourself up. This takes a long time to master, and you need to practice being a loving person.

In any case, it is best to rid yourself of toxic relationships and to establish a community of people who are loving, compassionate, and kind. Keep all aspects of your inner and outer environment as clean as you can and be organized in all of your endeavors.

During the time I was grieving the loss of my husband, I knew I wanted to find joy again. I also knew that I couldn't allow any negative people or situations in my life because I was already dealing with enough pain and trauma. I cut out news completely and anyone who wanted to tell me how to be and how to feel I left out of my life.

Instead, I started going into nature, watching comedies, and opening up to anything that brought relief like music and meditation. I even started on a spiritual quest in an effort to put light into the darkness in my heart. This helped me to eventually heal and reconnect with my joy.

Benefits of having a self-love practice

Love is redemptive and so enriching for your life. Society has focused on outward expression of love, loving your husband or your children and family. What is important is the love you give to yourself because it is only when you fill your own cup that you're able to share with others. Here are some of the benefits of having a self-love practice:

- You know who you are which means you do not need outside validation to be yourself. You're not going to feel love because of the number of likes or hearts on your social media post.

- You create healthy boundaries that will ensure you can truly be your best for whatever you commit yourself to do.

- You're always in harmony with yourself.

- You're content inside and out that is you don't sit waiting for someone else to come and validate you in order for you to feel valued.

- You use your energy for productivity and not to mourn and complain about events that are happening in your life.

- You feel connected with your Higher self and you trust your inner guidance.

- You give and receive love unconditionally

- You see innocence in other people

- You become a lover of truth, meaning you're not going to let fear dictate who you should be.

- You can express openly what you really want and share the real you.

- Your compassion grows and you can see beyond the fears and masks of others.You don't take life's challenges personally, instead you use the events that happen in your life to learn more about who you are and what is valuable to you.

Practicing self-love has amazing health benefits that it is important for all of us to start practicing it today. I would encourage you to start doing just one thing to show yourself love. You're a miracle that had a one in a million chance to be born. Appreciate your miraculous nature and be grateful for who you are. You were created out of pure love and you are loved. It is time for you to start believing it.

The Complexity and Psychology of Self-Esteem

Assessing self-esteem can be quite problematic. The issue lies in the fact that self-esteem can fluctuate on a moment-to-moment basis throughout the day. It is also often related to a role or function. Some people can have millions of euro or dollars while also battling social anxiety or depression.

Others are excellent at dating but awful at work. However, it is significant that the confidence lies in the person's perception of himself or herself in that particular field.

Self-esteem stems from our attachment to something. For example, a chef might take pride in his status as a wonderful cook. And if you were disappointed in the food, the chef would be very unhappy compared to somebody who does not cook for a living. The same applies to any person who is proud of the role that he or she is doing.

This is why self-love is on another level. It is not attached to anything. Because whenever you are attached to something

86

that is not your identification, your validation stems from what others think. Even when it is positive, it is still temporary. But self-love is non- dualistic and constant once you practice it.

Building Self-Esteem

There is no set routine for building self-esteem. While scientific studies have confirmed the benefits, they have been unable to provide a standardized means of improving self-esteem. This is because each human being is very complex and multifaceted.

There is a lot of interest in science these days to understand how the human being perceives reality and how it is associated with the past and the present. Researchers now understand the value of sleep and further inroads are yet to be made in researching dream sleep and its significance.

Many of the products and services designed to enhance self- esteem have the opposite effect of their stated purpose. People actually feel worse after taking them.

This is because these products and services tend to be

externally orientated, such as cosmetics, voice tonality, fancy clothes, and other superficial modalities. Even immersion can be difficult for those suffering from social anxiety and other issues. If a person is nervous speaking in front of a crowd, then forcing them to repeat this action could simply lead to a breakdown and further trauma.

On the flip side, there are definitely things that you can do. While there is no "one size fits all" approach that can help with self- esteem, every individual will respond well to certain healing modalities? The trick lies in finding out what the issue is and helping the individual to overcome it. This is what psychology and shadow work is all about.

The person is able to see the difficulties more clearly using dream work, journaling, direct communication, hypnosis, and other forms of therapy. Once these demons are brought to the light of consciousness, they can dissipate.

Unfortunately, it is a lot harder than it sounds and these ingrained tendencies do not simply dissipate in the majority of instances.

Figuring out Self-Esteem

There is a constant debate within the spiritual and psychological community with regard to the 'correct' way forward with self- esteem and with healing in general. Some push for positivity, others shadow work.

Some advocate integration, others say that 'letting go' is the best approach. Some state that balance and harmony are the ultimate pinnacles of healing, more dictate that creative chaos is the natural state of a universe that is constantly changing.

The fact is that all of these approaches will work at certain times for certain people. Some people might need to integrate the various parts of themselves, while others might really need to let go of issues. As always, the best way to build confidence in a person suffering from depression or low self-esteem of some sort is to let them communicate their feelings openly first and establish an open dialogue.

Instead of simply pushing therapy on the person, other

alternative therapies might be suggested for people who might benefit from them. It has to be their choice if it is to work.

Therefore, the person uses their own power and resources to come up with creative answers. It could be anything from painting to diet to meditation to going back to university to a number of the above at a time.

Practical Ways to Build Self-Esteem

As complex and multifaceted as building self-esteem might be, there are still a number of down to earth and practical ways to enhance it.

Taking yourself out of situations where you are not confident is equally as important as putting yourself in places where you have high levels of self-esteem.

The following are 7 practical ways to build self-esteem.

- **Put Your Health First** - Always put your health and wellbeing first. Nothing is more important than being stress-free in a healthy body. This will also involve a certain amount of discipline. Exercise regularly and stick mostly to a healthy diet and being in good health leads to good self-esteem. By looking and feeling better, people will also start to treat you better.

- **Save Money** - Regardless of your beliefs about money, you need it needed to function in the world. You should have a healthy amount of it at hand, so that you do not have to constantly worry about it. Save a certain amount of money and budget so that you always have enough for the bills in advance. Anxiety and stress over money takes up a lot of mental and emotional resources.

- **Build Competence** - Whatever your role is, make sure you are competent at it. Like a lack of money, if you worry about being able to perform your job then your well-being will suffer. Competence is one of the best things to assist in building confidence. Whatever you are good at, try to get better.

- **Focus** - Do not exert all of your resources trying to do too many things at once. Keep it simple and focus on doing one thing at a time. Many people overexert themselves with too many tasks or go the other way with too much vacation time. You can use focus to build money and competence slowly over time.

- **Meditation** - Health, money, and competence are the building blocks of a healthy human being. But after this, it is time to take it to the next level and build confidence that is hard to shake in any circumstance. Meditation can assist in detaching you from reality, so you are not as affected by the thoughts and opinions of others any more. It won't work overnight, but it definitely works if you persist with your practice.

- **Inner Assessment** - You need to identify core fears and beliefs that you have and find some way to work on them. There are online questionnaires, which can help you to identify what your beliefs are. You can use affirmations to help change these beliefs or work on them using physical activities.

- **Reframe** - Reframing is a great way to put yourself into a good mood. When something happens that you do not like, simply list the good that came out of it. Everything can be reframed, and everything is subjective in any case. Nobody sees the same situation in the same way. For example, when I was in secondary school there was a strike during our final exams. Something went wrong and part of our school burnt down. I had to move to Harare to go to school and that's where I met my Taurai, who became my husband. I don't know if I would've met him otherwise.

- **Sleep** – Many people are not aware of the impact lack of enough sleep has on mental health and well-being. I remember going through a period of insomnia while I was grieving. I couldn't think straight; my brain was foggy, and any minor issue would stress me out. Tiredness made me cranky and I would lash out at my family for minor infractions. If you have ever been, around babies, you know when they are irritable and cranky after eating then it's time for a nap, right? Taking the time to sleep is good body maintenance that ensures you function at your optimum level.

Mastering Thoughts and Emotions

There's no dispute within esoteric circles that the quality of your thoughts will determine the nature of your reality. Thought is really just a habit. If you can really change your thoughts, you will be able to control what you experience. Even if you end up in a negative environment, you can still control your reaction to it.

Moreover, a negative environment is most likely only negative because you have some kind of negative belief surrounding it, which you can change.

Mastering Thoughts

Thoughts gather momentum and tend to perpetuate themselves. So, the rich get richer and the poor get poorer on this planet not due to any kind of structured inequality, but simply due to thoughts of poverty perpetuating themselves and thoughts of riches perpetuating themselves. People prefer to adopt a victim mindset than to take control of their thoughts and focus continually on wealth and solutions. It is so much easier to blame a villain than to accept responsibility. It is also far lazier and accomplishes nothing at all.

The primary reason that people have not mastered their thoughts is not a lack of information. It is a lack of dedication and consistency. People have a habit of instantly reacting to negative news and events without understanding the power of their own minds.

They are the ones generating the stress, anxiety and worry because of what they focus on. Gaining power over your thoughts is a lifelong endeavor. It is the only real task that you have to do, as it determines everything.

Mastering Emotions

Thoughts and emotions are interlinked. While thoughts lead to emotions, it is entirely possible to learn to leverage emotions without any thoughts whatsoever. This is even more powerful.

It is not the thought that generates the power, but the emotional energy behind it. So, you can go directly to the source. Of course, the most powerful emotion is love, and you should try to master this as much as possible.

Love can be generated if you place loving thoughts on people that you adore. You can begin doing this by thinking about something you appreciate or admire about that person. Visualise them in your mind and send them good will thoughts. Over time, you will be able to summon the energy directly. This will not happen overnight, but it will greatly increase your power and charisma.

Some events can generate an immensely negative reaction from a person due to previous trauma. This can be very difficult to deal with as emotions are triggered. But the principles remain the same, though the intensity might be far worse. You have to find a way to deactivate the negative energy and focus on positive energy.

This does not mean that you are ignoring the problem. A

problem would imply that there is something wrong with you that needs to be fixed. Reality is perception, and you need to change your mental and emotional lens to see things from the perspective of the higher self - who you really are:

"We do not see things as they are; we see them as we are" (The Talmud)

A Note on Beliefs

Beliefs need to be examined to see where they came from and if they are true to you at all. They are often mentioned but rarely explored in detail because most people don't know how to change their beliefs even when their beliefs may be causing them not to reach their highest potential

A belief is simply a thought that has been repeated over and over again. It becomes ingrained in the human mind as a fact, though this is not really the case. Your life is a manifestation of your beliefs. Take the time to evaluate your life and see what your beliefs are. If you keep dating a person who causes you some emotional or physical harm, then you have a belief that this is how you should be treated in your relationships. These beliefs can be deactivated easily if you turn your attention toward positive thoughts. The new beliefs replace the old.

Again, it is not possible to feel both love and hate at the same time. They are opposites. If you have a belief about someone that results in the energy of hatred, then you will continue to have this belief unless the thought chain is interrupted. You need to know that you can choose to have a different belief.

Activating the exact opposite is key to deactivating a negative belief. However, you need to use meditation as an intermediary. If you are in anger or despair, first you need to meditate and slow down. Then you need to access the opposite belief.

Deep beliefs are often the biggest obstacle to new states of awareness. For example, you might have read all of the material but deep down do not feel you are worthy of a partner. Making a choice to let go of the belief and taking up a meditation practice will help you to overcome that belief.

There are a wide number of erroneous beliefs such as "resources are scarce and we must compete", "you have to work hard to get rich" and "all the good men are taken."

These beliefs are completely inaccurate, but your belief has the power to make them accurate for you. Everybody has their own set of beliefs which need to be scrutinized. It is not possible to evolve with limiting beliefs. You can use the power of habits to remove them over time.

The Power of Habits

The power of habits is not to be underestimated. A mature understanding of habits and how to use them is fundamental to becoming a whole and integrated human being. Because your habits are the primary determinant of whom you are, and who you become:

"Repetition of the same thought or action develops into a habit, which, repeated frequently enough, becomes an automatic reflex" (Vincent Norman Peel)

What you do every day will change who you are. The issue is that most people have poor habits, which they complete every day without thinking about them. Your habits will help you to correct some of your subconscious tendencies.

The Subconscious

Consider that more than half of all of your daily activities are automatic. You do not put any conscious awareness into them.

Habits are a way for our brains to conserve energy over time, and they are vital to our functioning. Imagine if you had to calculate every step to work beforehand, how to make your breakfast, open the front door, take each step to the car, start the ignition, drive in busy traffic etc. We don't store procedural memory in conscious memory but rather in subconscious memory.

Thankfully, our subconscious takes care of all of it. The brain is only capable of remembering between 5-9 facts at a time. The rest is passed to the subconscious for processing. When you do something once, you can complete it the next time around on autopilot far more easily. Most of your habits are driven by unconscious fears that you are not yet aware of. Correcting habits can have the effect of correcting these fears, though it takes time.

How to Master Habits

Everything that you do regularly is no more than a habit. Some habits are incredibly deeply ingrained. The longer that a habit is put in place, the harder it is to replace. Think of the example of a person who has been smoking for 30 years, constantly used to taking smoking breaks with friends and smoking at home.

It is just as easy to make a habit out of going to the gym or meditating as it is to smoke or drink alcohol.

As everybody knows, it is not the gym or meditation that is difficult. It is the thought of the gym or meditation and getting to the place itself. It is the mind resisting change because the brain wants what is familiar. Anything new is seen as a threat and is resisted intensely.

It takes 3 days for the body to get used to a different kind of diet. In drug rehabilitation, the first 3 days are the most difficult, and after this, the patient will have a much easier time staying away from drugs.

This is because the body is physically dependent on the drug and has adapted to its presence. After 3 days, it will have adapted to functioning without the drug. However, this is only the physical side of things.

Scientific studies have established that it takes 3 weeks for a habit to become ingrained. After 3 weeks, it is likely that the person will continue doing it afterwards. So, if you really want to master a habit, the 3 day and 21-day marks are the most important.

After these points, it will become a lot easier. Once you have installed a habit, it just becomes second nature. It does not really matter what it is. This is the beauty of habits once you understand them and use them to your benefit.

Of course, the ultimate habit that you want to maintain is positive thoughts. The minute you find yourself thinking of a negative thought, try to change it to something positive. Changing habits takes time and practice but with a bit of effort you will get better at it.

Overtime, even this will become second nature, and negative thoughts will become a thing of the past. This is the ultimate habit to adopt, so it is best to start with other practices such as meditation or diet first.

Good Habits to Master

Affirmations are one of the best ways to enhance self-esteem, as long as they are done correctly. However, it should be borne in mind that the affirmations need to be believable.

If the affirmations too far from where you are, then it won't be believed and will just remind you of what you are not. The affirmation also needs to be in the present tense and not a negation. "I am not poor" is reinforcing poverty, while "I am rich" reinforces riches. This is because the subconscious mind does not register the negative. I am not poor is understood as I am poor. Good examples of affirmations are; I can do this, I am capable, I am positive.

There is an infinite amount of habits to take on board, so you will need to be selective. The best habits will depend on the person in question. It could be meditating, drinking a smoothie, visualizing your perfect day, or just making your bed before work. Also, consider turning off your Wi-Fi at night and reducing technology usage before sleep.

The time just prior to sleeping and just upon waking is one where you have access to the theta state while still conscious. If you can try to manifest a positive emotion in these states, your day and night will run much more smoothly.

Lucid dreaming is another modality you can use to help you get what you want. The morning is the best time to complete a task or engage in a positive habit. Studies have demonstrated that willpower is highest in the morning and tends to wane as the day goes on.

So, start your day off as well as you possibly can. The worst thing that you can do is roll out of bed, look at your emails, shower, grab a slice of toast, and head to work.

When you are looking at your emails, you are downloading stress first thing in the morning. The morning time is sacred, and you need to keep some space there for relaxation. Sadly, most people are stressed about work and do not even give themselves the morning to relax. You might think that you don't have time, but you can make time by getting up 20 or 30 minutes earlier. The cumulative benefits will amaze you.

Habits are Hard

Whatever kind of habit you adopt, remember to stick with it for at least 3 weeks. Practice doing it first thing in the morning.

Over time, it will become second nature to you. Incorporate your habits one at a time so you do not get overwhelmed.

Habits are very difficult to break out of once they become ingrained. They are ingrained so strongly in the brain that they can even survive brain damage.

On the other hand, this can be a good thing if you adopt positive habits. As per Warren Buffett:

"The chains of habit are too light to be felt until they are too heavy to be broken"

As difficult as habits may be to break, if you stick with the process of starting something new you will get better at it and the benefits can be phenomenal. You can find yourself on a never-ending spiral of self-development. One habit after the next can be broken, from the smallest to the biggest.

People often need to identify one keystone habit that will result in a change in all the others. You can use the power of habit to find your true self and establish unshakable self-esteem.

Creative Ways to Boost Self- Love

Meditation, organization, discipline, purification, diet and more have huge benefits. These processes can be very stale and lifeless for many people, despite their necessity. You do not have to stick to these aesthetic practices. In fact, loving yourself is anything but boring. It should be the most enjoyable journey of a lifetime.

Because you are literally doing things that make you happy at high intensity. Taking action in giving yourself love is so satisfying you will wonder why you haven't been doing it already.

Creativity and Imagination

Creativity is a means of accessing parts of you that have been lying dormant due to societal conventions. As stated in the beginning, we shut down our creative, spiritual, emotional and physical centers due to the pressure to conform. I used to love laying with my legs up against the wall. Of course, I would do this in my bedroom, and I stopped because this was not how young girls were supposed to sit even though this used to relax me. This was actually a Yoga pose my body knew how to do and now I have to relearn the skill. Hah! Go figure.

The challenge lies in opening up these faculties at a later stage. When your body compels you to do something, do it because maybe your body is directing you to do what it needs.

The hallmarks of self-love are authenticity and originality. Creativity can only come from inside of you. This makes it difficult for other people to understand and accept what you feel compelled to do. Some people think if you do something unique then you're an outcast. This mentality has turned people into copycats and followers in order to fit in.

People copy each other all the time. Think of the number of online books on "how to make money online". The same old advice repeated and sold over and over and over. It is not possible to make money online by simply taking another person's formula and repeating it. You need to be original to be truly successful. This is why you should stay away from other people's formulas for success but instead search for what works for you. Even if they genuinely worked for the original creator, they might not work for you because they are not your creation.

This is an important point.

The Universe only whispers to you, your calling and your purpose. Only you can do it that way. When you wield your power and follow your instincts then you live the life of your purpose.

Creative Practices

One of the biggest and most powerful ways to boost self-love is to go on a wild trip. Do something that you have never done before. This will help you discover who you really are and what you're capable of achieving.

Better yet, do something that is far outside of your comfort zone, like quit your job and travel the world. This is guaranteed to open up previously inaccessible avenues of thought and emotion that you never knew you had. When my husband Taurai and I left Zimbabwe and moved to Ireland, we had no idea what to expect in our daily lives. It was so unimaginable that we really didn't think about it. I learnt that I am calm under pressure, I am not afraid to ask for help and I am very resourceful.

I discovered that I am good with people even if I don't know them personally. Knowing who I am keeps me grounded and other people's opinions of me have nothing to do with me. There is nothing more disappointing than travelling down the same road with a few variations because we all want to grow and we can only do that by discovering new experiences, ideas and methods.

Wage increases and other titles are immensely boring to people who are living their true lives. They are typically no more than abstractions that people use to content themselves with very unsatisfying lives.

There is a variety of ways to improve your imagination. Bear in mind that it is an ongoing and never-ending process, but one that gets more satisfying as times goes by.

The best practices include:

- Creative writing.

- Art.

- Martial arts.

- Dancing.

- Singing.

- Cooking.

- Travel.

- Making something, painting, crotchet, drawing, colouring, whatever floats your boat

- Anything else that you love to do.

Obviously, the list is not exhaustive. There is room for creativity in logical subjects such as accounting or math. However, it has to be applied dynamically and used often by the person. Otherwise, the imagination will lie dormant as the person continues to rely on textbooks and manuals written by somebody else. The way to enhance creativity lies in persistence. If you are painting, then you need to try and paint every single day. You will have certain insights and eureka, moments now and again, but you cannot tell when they are going to happen.

Regardless of what creative activity you are doing, you need to engage with it regularly. Creativity can also help to uproot subconscious tendencies. This is meant to be a fun practice, so you don't need to seek perfection. Take it as a way to play and discover your creativity.

For example, characters in a story or images in a painting are reflected in the inner psyche. While you may not be able to discuss such things in public, they can be expressed through creative means.

Dr Brené Browne, in her book, *"Daring greatly"*, talks about the importance of taking part in creative activities as essential to wellbeing and happiness. Tapping into your deep recesses and coming out with something beautiful is great for your imagination. The more you use it, the better it gets. Human beings were born to create. Tapping into your creativity helps, you learn how to solve everyday problems creatively. Remember, there's no wrong way or right way to create so you're not going to fail at it.

If you happen to be a creative person who succeeds so much that you make a career out of it, author, musician, painter and many others, remember that the work you do is a way for you to express yourself. Therefore, other people's critique should not be your problem. I have heard of musicians who quit producing music because they felt or heard from critics that their work was not as good as their earlier or more successful work. Don't listen to people who are not in the ring fighting. They don't know what it takes to do what you do and besides you do it for your soul and other people just benefit.

Intuition

The intuition is an incredibly underappreciated aspect of every individual. Your intuition if relied upon will develop and grow over time. This helps make your life much easier as you rely on a higher power to help you with life's problems. Your intuition can answer every question you can ever come up with, if you're willing to listen to the answer.

Using your intuition will free you from the stress of strenuous mental thought. You need to detach from too much reasoning and trust your gut instinct as guidance from your intuition may appear not to make sense at a rational level and yet things always work out for the better.

The conscious mind is very limited and can only process a small amount of information at a time.

Intuition, creativity, and imagination are tightly linked. The processes that you can use to increase creativity are the same ones that you can use to increase your intuitive power. Intuition is your biggest friend when it comes to making life choices. There are thousands of ways to increase self-love, but only a few will be perfect for you at a specific time.

Following your intuition, is a lot easier than people make it out to be. You get better at it through practice. If you feel compelled to do something and your gut tells you it's going to work, then go for it even when other people might not be supportive. They can't listen in to what is being whispered to you.

Don't dismiss your desires and goals as irrelevant. They are the single greatest signposts that you have. Above all, find something that you love to do and be creative in doing it. This is your true self, and this is empowering.

If you love yourself, give yourself the gift of doing what you love 24/7 without caring what other people think of you. It is the pinnacle of human achievement to be uniquely you without input from anyone else.

Concluding thoughts on Self-Love

Finding out who you really are and generating self-love for yourself is the most rewarding experience that you can have.

The spiritual term is self-realization and is beyond the understanding of those who have not experienced it.

Yet some people more than others will exhibit higher levels of self-esteem. After all, confidence is simply being more aligned with who you really are. The people who try to be something they are not are the ones who are under-confident and underneath it all, they are not being authentic, and they know it.

It takes a remarkable amount of resources and energy to put up a facade and it is immensely energizing when you align yourself with your own Divinity.

In the words of the Greeks:

"Know thy self and you shalt know the Gods and all the universe"

Part 3 –

True Love

True Love

Do you know what true love is?

Have you ever found true love?

For some, these questions are quite hard to answer.

True love is not easily acquired and felt because over time we have become very good at hiding from it. We have spent most of our human existence putting love in a box because it scares us what love can make us do. We feel better when we put limitations on what love is because then we feel as if we can control it. Love comes in a variety of types.

Like others, you can say that you are loved if your family shows their affection to you. Love can be affection between friends, parents and their children, people and their pets, man and woman, and many other romantic liaisons. Marianne Williamson said, "it *is not our darkness that scares us but our light.*"

You may also feel the same way if you are attracted to your opposite gender. Love has two sides – the willingness to love and willingness to love back.

Love is not only for your family, partner or any special person. It is very limiting to think you can only love 5 or so members of your family and no one else. The truth is the more you love the bigger your capacity to love grows. You can also show love for God, country, surroundings and a lot more.

Love is a short but powerful word. It protects nurtures, endures and brings people together. It also sets people free and finds life, honor and prosperity.

Love can be just like a sense of what heaven will be like. However, love is not just, what makes the world go round. It is what makes the ride so worthwhile.

Once you utter the word "I Love You", always ensure that you really mean it. It means that once you love someone, you have to give everything to them. You can't love and be afraid at the same time. For example, if you say you love someone and yet you hold back a part of yourself or something about yourself then you really don't love them. Giving everything means opening up and revealing your true self at all times. It is always telling the truth.

At present, finding true love seems quite tough because most people are hiding, too afraid to reveal who they really are. Love will push your buttons and test your limits. Being honest and telling the truth about what your values are is the only way to find your true love. You might be thinking that you will be too vulnerable but if you love yourself first this will not be an issue for you. Love is the only thing worth living for.

Whether you are young or not, you can find true love. Strangely enough, love also makes us feel young and connects us to our younger playful selves.

So, how can you do it? To find true love, you need to consider various things. You have to understand yourself first and know what really makes you happy.

Since love is the root of real happiness and success, you

have to understand how to find true love. You should also know the different facts about this broad term.

The main question is, is true love easy to find? Like others, can you find the real love you are looking for? Over the next few pages, you will learn what true love is and how you can find and hold onto it!

Why People Are Lacking Love?

Lack of love is the common problem in every relationship. Understanding its causes can be a remarkable help in learning to love again, getting in touch with others and finding true love. Past fears and hurts may be having more of an impact on your current relationships.

So, why are people lacking love? If you don't know the reason why, then, start exploring now!

There are several reasons why people are lacking love.

If you are not familiar with some of the multiple reasons, here they are:

- **Childhood Trauma** – If you have experienced trauma during your childhood, it can be a great cause of your inability to love. Say for instance, if you feel that you are not being loved since birth, you will never learn to love yourself. You also don't have an idea about true love. This is usually the case if your parents or primary caregivers experienced trauma in childhood themselves.

Recently, the science of epigenetics has discovered that we pass on cellular memories of trauma and other experiences to the next generations. Some scientists have gone on to say decreased methylation can go on for seven generations. Trauma is harmful to your biological, emotional and spiritual wellbeing.

Your legacy is not passed on through the wealth and knowledge you leave behind but it is passed on from both parents to children and onwards to their own children. Healing that trauma is the only way to ensure you and your descendants will have the happy, thriving relationship you want for them. Healing trauma is also to ensure the emotional, biological and spiritual well-being of your descendants.

- **Lack of Self-Confidence** – If you keep on having negative thoughts about yourself, you can't easily find true love. Like others, you are not convinced that you are worthy to be loved and treasured. In addition, low self-esteem can also lead you to believe that the more people try to show you that you are valuable, the more you doubt them. Love is not something you're given. The love you feel for another or from another is only what is inside of you. When you allow it to rise and grow, then you feel the emotions and feelings associated with love. Your body will release the associated bonding hormones and you'll feel like you're on top of the world.

- **Seeking Revenge** – This is also another reason why people are lacking love. If their hearts are full of anger and revenge, they will never find peace and real love. Though someone shows concerns and affection to them, they will ignore them. I have met some clients that are still keeping grudges towards people who moved on 20 years ago. The worst part is they take out their anger on the men they meet and after a while, the men give up and walk away. Revenge doesn't help anyone because all that negative angst will just mess up your own energy field.

- **Believing that True Love Doesn't Exist** – If a person

thinks this way, they will never waste their time finding what true love is. They will never value the love of other people. They will also prefer to protect themselves rather than show their feelings to other people. You manifest in your life what you believe. It goes without saying that if you believe love doesn't exist then you will never experience it. If it does show up in your life you will accredit it to something else. I have met people in my life that are afraid of being loved. You show them love and kindness and they run in the opposite direction. Allowing them to make this choice for themselves is a way of showing love to them and to yourself for not forcing something that is not going to work.

- **Feel that They Can Live Alone** – Some people think that they don't need anyone in their lives. For them, they can live in this world without asking for any love or affection from other people. With this perception, they prefer to be alone. This is okay as long as they don't start to change their mind as they grow older and their partying days are far behind when loneliness sets in. Many people regret not making an effort to find someone to love.

Love is the connecting energy between God and human. When that connection is made, unity of all beings becomes reality. As a result, love defeats all anger and other negative feelings. If you want to find real love, simply read the succeeding paragraphs.

Steps in Finding a True Love

Step 1: Don't Make it your Identity

This does not mean you cannot talk to a therapist or explain a bad situation that happened. It means your reaction doesn't perpetuate the trauma or negative experience. I'm sure you know someone who was maybe in an abusive relationship and they got out. They use every opportunity they get to describe all the bad things that were done to them.

They also use that experience to avoid healing and moving on to a happier life. You have the power to choose your words. You can't choose how other people behave but you can choose how you react or what perspective you take and the words you use. Take the events that happen in your life as just events and not the description of your life. I realized early on that most of my girlfriends and other female acquaintances spent their time criticizing men.

They never really had anything nice to say about men and sometimes called them dogs. I decided at the time to only say the good things Taurai did and handle our issues privately. I never ignored behaviours that annoyed me, but I also didn't take them personally. I knew while he might have said something upsetting, his intention was never to hurt me. I have found that this helped our relationship not have ongoing niggling issues.

Step 2: Be Responsible for Your Feelings - Whether you like it or not, you have the complete power on how you react to all situations and choose how you feel. When I took responsibility for my own happiness, I felt so much freedom. I didn't have to react to how my husband was feeling. Initially I used to think when he was angry, it was because of something I did or didn't do. Can you see how disempowering that could be? When I started taking charge of my own happiness, I let go of the responsibility to make him happy.

As it turned out, Taurai was frustrated about his work situation and it had nothing to do with me. By releasing the need to make him happy and instead taking responsibility for making myself happy, my husband didn't have the burden to make me happy too, so his burden and responsibilities lessened. He became a much happier person to live with. Since you are responsible for your feelings, it is your choice whether you want to feel good or not.

Step 3: Love Needs Acceptance and Allowing People to be What They Are– It means that if you want to change someone, they have the right to inform you to change.

If you accept them for who they are, it means that you love them. I am not sure what it is, but many women choose a man who is almost the right match and then they set out to change him. They will try to beat him into shape, and he will resist. He will walk away from her if he feels strongly about who he is as a man, or he will succumb. The moment he does succumb, she loses respect for him and dumps him or divorces him or stays in a lifeless negative marriage. Ladies make sure the man you're choosing has the qualities that you like, and you can live with those that you don't like. When you find yourself trying to change a man, ask yourself where that inclination is coming from.

One of the signs of love is when who they are is good enough for you. Knowing no one is perfect but even his or her little habits are cute to you. That is a sign you love someone.

Step 4: Understand the Human Nature of Selfishness – If you know about this concept, you will learn how to be happy without expecting anything in return. You will also get the most and that is the joy of giving and seeing someone else happy.

I once met a couple that was always in competition. If he got her a present, she got him a bigger one. This isn't love, it is a competition.

Step 5: Always Remind Yourself about Positive Vibes – Whether you go and whatever you do, always guide yourself into a good path. Before making any move, try to know what the results of your actions will be.

I used to be so afraid of my husband cheating or doing something I didn't like. To avoid getting hurt I was very harsh and had lots of rules he had to follow. I didn't want him to mess with me, does that sound familiar? I started noticing that being in that mode didn't make me feel good. I wanted to have good vibes all the time, so I decided to let go of my need to control him and everything else. Interestingly we connected at a deeper level and he became more committed to our relationship and me.

Through practicing having good vibes you should expect that you can easily find your true love. People are attracted to positive people. So, start finding your true love now! Then, see how true-love changes your life. Through finding true love, you will learn how to live with great happiness.

What Is True Love?

Most people are very eager to know what true love is. Regardless of their age, they always wanted to experience the feelings of being loved and to show their affection to other people.

However, when you say true love, it doesn't only pertain to the man and woman who are in love with each other. It is also not only about the love between a mother and child.

True love is the best thing that can happen to someone. It is something much more than falling in love. It is faithful, pure, responsible, trustworthy, kind, loyal and unconditional.

True Love is:

- **Caring** – There are several forms of love. The typical examples of these are passion, virtuous, general affection and affection for the family. No matter how you defined love, they hold the same trait. That trait is caring. Caring is wanting the best for you at all times. They want you to be

134

the best version of you that you can be, and they want you to be happy all the time. They support your growth, pursuits and dreams. They also call you on things you might not be doing for your wellbeing.

- **Attached** – This attachment comes after the preliminary attraction like the mother and child bond. It is the long term that appears anywhere into a romantic relationship. Once you are attached with your mother, you will do everything to make her happy and that's the sign of love. Attachment also happens in romantic relationships when you release the bonding hormone, Oxytocin.

- **Attractive** – Chemistry and attraction forms a bond that allows people to mate through a romantic desire for another person. For a romantic relationship to survive there has to be a physical attraction as well. This is what distinguishes it from the other relationships with friends, siblings, workmates, parents, etc. Men and women unite as one physically and spiritually.

- **Committed** - If your partner loves you and you love him back, you are showing a real affection. A commitment is a dedication to you and to your relationship. Once a couple is committed to each other emotionally, spiritually and physically they usually move on to make their commitment public through an engagement or wedding. These days some people just profess to each other and themselves that, they are committed to each other without the need for a formal ceremony.

- **Intimate** – Intimacy is considered as the essential component of all relationships.

  To know your partners, you have to share your stories with them. It can be an effective way of bonding and showing that you trust them. Intimacy is a way of showing your true self to your partner including, weaknesses, strengths, dreams, ambitions and even fears. There's no hiding a part of yourself. You can only be truly intimate when you know who you are.

Loyalty- Commitment also requires loyalty. Loyalty is what builds trust and it cements the commitment. Loyalty should come from the heart and not from a contract. If you find you need a contract then there's no loyalty in your relationship. It is one of the ingredients required to maintain a relationship. You cannot be loyal to your partner without being loyal to yourself. That means being true to yourself first. How you feel and think is of paramount importance to build a deep level of loyalty in a relationship.

How to Identify True Love?

There are two keys to identify true love. These are the following:

- Be Completely Honest with Yourself – To find real love, you have to start with yourself. You have to know what you really want and what makes you happy. You need to know your values, your triggers and what matters to you. You also need to know what makes you angry and even what makes you sad. If you are honest with yourself, expect that you will find true love and real happiness.

- Understand the Level of Commitment with True Love – If you know the levels of commitment with true love, you can easily determine why you are showing affection to other people. Commitment is dedication. Dedication to their wellbeing, love, safety and happiness. You don't have to take responsibility for their happiness, but you have to notice and encourage them to do things that make them happy. That means you have to relinquish the need to be the top priority of their attention all the time.

Since the meaning of true love is quite broad, you have to understand it very well. Though its concepts are too comprehensive, it doesn't mean that you can't easily find the real definition of true love. Depending on your situations, you can easily define what true love is.

The one thing we don't usually talk about is that true

love is unconditional. This means, you don't just love someone because they are doing what you think is right. It means you love them even when they are frustrating and annoying you. It means you will commit to your relationship in order for both of you to win in the relationship. You have to allow them to grow as they need to, and they need to let you grow as you need to as well. This calls for patience, kindness and compassion.

If you're in a relationship just to please yourself then you're not ready for a real true love relationship. If you're in a relationship just to please the other person then you're not yet in a true love relationship. True love allows you to create a partnership of equals who value and support each other.

Traditional Love Ideas vs. New Age Ideas

Ideas about love become even broader as time passes by. Though the ideas of love are quite comprehensive, you don't have to be confused.

Whether old or modern times, you can easily understand what love is. To know more traditional and new age love ideas, here are the things you need to consider:

During old times, people had a concrete meaning of love. Once they felt something different or felt concern for another person, they assumed that they were in love. Sometimes it was based on how unique the person was compared to the other people around.

Here are some concepts of traditional love:

• Unity of the Two Lovers – Before and even during these days, people prefer to get married to make public their commitment to each other. People who fall in love with each other desire to unite as one through the Sacrament of

Matrimony.

•   Believe in the Existence of Cupid – Before, people believed in the existence of magic. Most women believed that true love will come their way when Mr. Cupid finds an ideal man for them.

•   Practice Courtly Love - Love pertains to courtship and courtesy. But it is not necessarily related to the institution of marriage. Most people also believe that love is an intense and passionate relationship between two partners.

These traditional love ideas or practices are also observed even in the present times. However, there are some adjustments. Say for instance, courting is becoming easier because of modern technologies. Before, men used traditional schemes to show their love.

Depending on their culture, they can follow their own practices. These practices were very strict and sometimes restricting. Couples didn't get the chance to know each other well before they made the marriage commitment.

New Age Love Ideas

Like traditional love ideas, most people believe in the Sacrament of Matrimony. However, because of the changes of law, some countries allow couples to file an annulment or divorce. This is often observed if the couples are not happily married.

If you are single, you will also notice that the courtship of traditional love ideas is different to present times. At present, men and women are using mobile devices to contact each other. They can also show their feelings with the use of social networking sites. Though there are some differences between traditional and new age love ideas, the concept of love is still there.

Whether you are following the traditional or modern schemes, you will never be tired of showing how you value your loved ones. Although traditional practices were more restrictive and limited, people clearly understood the courtship process and actions. Today we have more freedom and less structure, and this can be confusing for some people but the principles of love still apply.

Self-Empowerment

Empowerment is the quickening power that moves you to do things that you never thought you could do. It is life changing and a key for your dreams.

Empowerment resides in your spirit. It is just like a hidden treasure that longs to be found. So, what does empowerment for love mean to you?

Empowerment for love is doing things for attracting and binding marriage opportunities, boosting your bonds of marriage and finding real love and happiness. It is waking up to reality like I did that my marriage was not making me happy. It is opening up to what is possible even though I didn't know how to create it yet.

Like others, loving yourself is on the path towards empowerment. Most people talk about loving themselves and this is the first step not the final aim.

How can you love yourself?

- Stop Criticizing Yourself Every Day – Instead of doing this; think of positive things about yourself. You also need to remember things and situations that make you feel happy. This can help you see that you are lovable person.

- Stop Thinking Negative Thoughts – Everyone experiences difficulties in life. When facing complicated issues, make sure that you always acknowledge your emotions and choose to find something helpful in the situation. Through changing your mind's perceptions, you will attract positive vibes in your life. You will also see that various people are willing to help you to overcome your situations.

- Treat Yourself Like You Desire Others to Treat You - If you think that you are not worthy to be loved, then, other people may also think the same way. Just remember that you have good qualities that most people admire. So, start noticing those qualities and mold them.

- Learn to Love Negative Things in Your Life - Unlike others, don't let the negative things bring you down. You can use them as your motivation to go after your dreams and achieve them. The death of my husband motivated me to do more with my life and now I help women transform their relationships into more fulfilling experiences. If someone says that you are not worthy to be loved, then, prove to them that you have the best qualities and you can live as happy as others.

• Look in the Mirror and Praise Yourself – To empower your love, you have to begin in yourself. You have to know your qualities that make you an even better person. Through saying "I Love You" to yourself, you can achieve wonders. It can make you feel comfortable and full of confidence all the time. It helps you to stop being needy which is a quality that destroys a lot of relationships.

Aside from the above mentioned, you have to love yourself unconditionally. Like others, you are born unique. It means that there is no one else in this world just like you. You are so rare that there was a one in a million chance of the right sperm and the right egg getting together to produce you. You have to be grateful for that miracle alone every day of your life. This is the reason why you have to learn to love yourself. Through this, you will also learn how to love other people.

Once you value yourself, you will also see others as being equally valuable. This is why we dive so deep into self-love – it holds the key to everything. Without it, true love is but just a fleeting wish.

Concluding thoughts on True Love

Life is incomplete without love. Love can make your world go round. Without love, you will never be happy. Love teaches you to understand how to value yourself, other people, the environment and other things that surround you.

If you don't know how to love, you will be lonely. You also won't have a chance to mingle with other people. Loneliness has become one of the biggest health problems of the modern age despite technology connecting us to almost everyone in the world 24/7. If you are filled with anger and other negative thoughts, you will miss out on positive experiences because like attracts like. You cannot attract positive experiences while you're nurturing negative thoughts, it's against the law.

You will not understand why most people are happy while having a night out with their friends, bonding with their families and a lot more.

Like I've mentioned multiple times, to find true love, you have to begin inside yourself. You should know how to love yourself before anybody else. The main question is, how can you do it? To love yourself, you should give yourself a chance. You should see the good in you.

It means that you have to learn to let go and move on with your life. You also need to forgive mistakes committed by others. However, when it comes to your own mistakes, you will surely find it hard to accept the reality. So, what you need to do is to learn to find what went wrong and how to correct it. Sometimes correcting it is just to surrender.

It is an excellent idea and much better than keeping on judging or blaming yourself. In addition, you can love yourself through giving continuous compliments. Words are very powerful, and it is one way of boosting your self-confidence. You just need to express how you feel about yourself in front of the mirror.

If you love yourself, you can start loving other people around you. You can show affection to your friends, relatives or someone you like. However, being self-centered can bring negative results. This is often observed if you keep on doing things that can make you happy while affecting the rights of other people. If you want to be happy, make sure that you love without hurting other people. Real love ensures that other people have the same rights and allowances as yourself. Anything else is not real love.

You can't wait to find your true love? Then, just relax and you will just realize that the person you are looking for is right beside you. You just need to open your heart and mind. Then, you will finally see what true love is. Don't allow the tall, dark and handsome myth of romantic novels stop you from identifying the person who is loving you every day who is right next to you. This is because we tend to take our loved ones for granted.

Part 4 –

Relationships

Relationships

Look at your hands. The four gaps between your fingers were made for your special someone to fill. However, being in a relationship is not always a bed of roses. Sooner or later, both of you will encounter problems, challenges or conflict. Thus, there is a tendency that either of you will let go of the hand of the other.

Challenges in a relationship are a wakeup call that helps you to recommit to your relationship and expand your capacity for love.

Because, we don't like pain, when a relationship becomes too taxing most of us run away. It's just like taking a painkiller when you have a headache. You don't want to know the source of the pain, you just want it gone. Going deeper and understanding the source of your dissatisfaction or conflict will help you to grow and transform your relationship for the better. Most of us were never taught how to handle conflict that's why we attack those who don't think, feel or look like us. We react with violence. What if you choose to wade in the mud and find out why you're reacting the way you are and why your spouse is resistant? What if you hold on and find a solution together that makes both of you feel good? Wouldn't that be amazing?

Your Love Life

When you have found the love of your life, you feel like everything is perfect, right? That is how magical love is. It can turn a gray world into a colorful one, a frown into a smile and melt a frozen cold heart.

In the sonnet *My Love is Life to Ice* by Edmund Spenser, he describes love as something that can alter the course all of human kind. To put it simply, it can dramatically change your life.

However, nothing stays the same. Given the fact that nothing in this world lasts forever, something will surely change in the way you and your partner feel somewhere in time. These changes are caused by problems, which are triggered either by internal or external factors. Internal factors are caused by a change of perception of feeling towards your partner while external factors are caused by third party, money, misunderstandings on a certain matter, jealousy, contradicting beliefs in politics, religion, etc. and others.

If you are wondering on how breakups and divorce come to be, then these factors are the culprits. However, it is up to you and your partner if you are going to let those assail your relationship or not.

Do you feel guilty because you are the one who made a mistake, or do you find it hard to forgive your partner because you feel betrayed? These instances will really cloud your mind and heart with confusion, but if you do the right thing, in the end you will not be haunted by the wrong choices you have made. Isn't it surprising that divorce and breakups cause a lot of lasting pain and yet most people don't make the effort to find a solution that will keep them together?

Is your relationship currently hanging by a cliff? Do you

want to hold on to it? Well, as long as the waters cover the sea and as the sun rises in the east and sets in the west, it is not too late. You just need to have a good relationship rescue plan that will help you save your love life. Norman Vincent Peale, in his book, *"The power of positive thinking,"* describes a woman who went to him in desperation because her husband was going to begin divorce proceedings in thirty days.

He advised the young woman to focus on what she wanted and visualize herself being happy in the relationship with her husband. Sure enough, within thirty days they had restored their relationship to a loving one. She used the power of visualization to restore her relationship to its original sparkle. You also have the power to visualize which means you can reignite your own relationship.

Often people make mistakes in a relationship and bring this learning to their next relationship. If you work on it, this learning can apply in the existing relationship. Don't make the mistake of training other people's husbands. I know of a couple where the wife was complaining constantly because the husband was not house trained, for example he never cleaned after himself nor did any household chores. In time, he started to do chores and she left him because she said, "*if he knew how to do it, why wasn't he doing it all this time?*" Maybe he didn't know the importance of doing chores because of his background but at least he was willing to learn. Anyway, he's now married to someone else who's benefiting from his awakening.

If you are able to make the right choices and keep your life on track, you can restore happiness in your relationship. To start rescuing the relationship, you need to come to terms with yourself. The following chapters will show you how.

Importance of a Healthy Relationship

In Creation, God made man first. Upon seeing that he was lonely, he created woman next. This only illustrates that men and women are meant to enjoy each other's company and to build a healthy relationship. What does a healthy relationship mean and why is it important?

Healthy Relationship

A healthy relationship means that you and your partner exercise a give and take process. With this, everything will stay in balance and neither of you will feel deprived of something because you fill each other's needs. Also, you can say that your relationship is really healthy if you and your partner work as a team or have created a partnership.

Always remember that it takes two to tango. In other words, you need to cooperate and work hard in everything that concerns your relationship.

A healthy relationship also depends on you and your

157

partner's health. This is not limited to physical health; in fact, this aspect is of low significance for a healthy relationship. Spiritual and mental health are actually the most influential elements that contribute to the health of any relationship. You have to know that your relationship is as healthy as the least healthy of you.

For example, if one of you has self-loathing, addicted to drugs, alcohol, sex or whatever issue you will both suffer the consequences of the other spouse's unhealthy choices.

Spiritual Health

Typically, most people link spirituality with religion. What they do not know is that there is a big difference between the two. The former is linked to how a certain person treats others while the latter is concerned with religious practices, rituals and traditions.

If you are loving and kind to others, then that only indicates that you are sound spiritually. However, if you mistreat people and take advantage of their weaknesses, then that means that you have poor spiritual health. Given that a relationship is the growth and unified interaction of two persons, each person's spiritual health is essential.

The most interesting thing with regard to spiritual health is that those who are not spiritually sound will commonly find themselves partnered with people who are not mentally sound. This kind of coupling may lead not only unhealthy, but leads to a toxic relationship. It is common for people to lean on the shoulder of someone else when they get depressed and to open up to those who increase the negative energy they emanate. This is the most destructive kind of relationship for both individuals.

Meanwhile, people with sound spiritual and mental health may find themselves with a person who lacks in either aspect, and they will remove themselves from this unhealthy relationship as quickly as possible. If they fail to do so, they will start to drain their very own health until they complement the deficiency of their partner. This kind of personal sacrifice will cause resentment on both sides in the end.

Understanding these fundamental foundational concepts will give you pathway to experience a healthy relationship, not only with your romantic partner, but with your friends, schoolmates, family and co- workers as well.

From time to time, do you find yourself in an unhealthy relationship? If yes, then it is about time to do some self-reflection.

Concentrate on your mental health. If you have an inability to examine yourself, it is ideal to get some help from trusted friends, family or experts.

The most crucial thing to bear in mind is that if you wish to experience a healthy relationship, you must be healthy yourself.

You cannot rely on someone else to do it for you. People with sound health will not choose to stay in a relationship with someone unhealthy. If you find yourself in a relationship with an abusive person, narcissist or someone emotionally unwell it means you have a deficiency inside of you that you need to address. You attract that which is familiar to you. This is the point of this book, to help you work on yourself so that you can attract the person you really want in your life.

If you have the ability to bring a healthy individual to an unhealthy level, then it will not lead to a strong and healthy relationship. Thus, it is important to fix your broken parts until you can confidently and happily smile at yourself in front of the mirror.

Always remember the golden rule, respect yourself and do not allow other people to use you or take advantage of your weaknesses. Have the willingness to help someone without expecting anything in return. When you are able to do that, you will sooner or later find yourself with a person that has the same attitude with you. In turn, both of you will experience the strongest, most incredible and healthiest relationship ever.

Mental Health

Mental health is how a person treats and views himself. It is true that this kind of health is commonly influenced by external stimuli, but it still depends on how a person responds to those stimuli towards him/herself. Again, this is why we began with self-love. I hope that you understand just how important it is by now.

It is how that person reacts, matures and grows from those experiences that gauge his/her mental health. By simply looking at it in that way, it is easier to perceive how essential mental health is to a sound relationship.

If a person does not have a sound relationship with him/herself, then he/she will not be able to contribute to a healthy and lasting relationship with anyone else. Another way of looking at it is, the way you feel about all the relationships in your life is a reflection of how you feel about yourself. It is a mirror of how you feel inside. Don't use this to beat yourself up but rather to focus on areas that need healing inside you.

So, why is a healthy relationship important? Actually, there are several reasons, and the pages of this book would not be enough to enumerate and explain them.

In a nutshell, a healthy relationship is very important simply because it will make you a better person and you can make the lives of others better too. You can't give what you don't have. When people learn to love themselves, they will love the people around them in return. What you give is what you will receive.

As a result, the world will be a better place to live in.

Showing Love in a Relationship

In the quest to be able to establish a strong and loving relationship the two of you need to learn all the various ways and actions that clearly get the message of love and concern across. You can learn any skill you want and the more you practice is the better you get at using it. Even love is learnable skill.

The following are some of the very basic ways to clearly show the message of love across to the other person through actions:

Show It

The simplest form of trying to show affection and love without coming on too strong would be the physical contact made whenever you're in each other's company. This could be as simple as holding hands or as protective and intimate as a kiss. A casual arm on the shoulder of the other person while walking or even sitting is also another non-invasive way of expressing

164

love. You also have to understand that men and women show love differently.

Lack of awareness may cause unnecessary conflict, for example a man going out to work and bringing money home is his way of showing love, while a woman might think if he does all that work but doesn't say the words that he loves her then he really doesn't love her.

Snuggling up together when relaxing is also a good way to show love and affection towards each other.

This is especially welcomed when both of you are not otherwise distracted or occupied. Some couples take this a step further by whispering loving, complimenting or other positive words into each other's ears.

This action is certainly one that illustrates intimacy and love. Mentioning how much they are missed when apart is also something most loving couples would express.

Taurai and I used to send each other text messages or one-line emails during the day after we were married, just to say hi. I didn't get upset if he didn't reply immediately because he could've been in the middle of a project. His replies when they came always made me smile.

Taking the time to do things for each other without being asked is a great way to show love. The other person would certainly feel loved and appreciated when you extend such actions to them without any prompting. Take time to notice the little things that your husband does for you and acknowledge them. It is also important to think about the different ways men and women show love because you might overlook some of the effort he's making.

This will give them a sense of value and certainly help them see the loving action as a sign of commitment and care. Taurai loved beans and I really didn't. I cooked beans for him regularly and I found that adding spices and other enhancers helped so that we could share the meal together.

I have to add, as your relationship grows you might observe another couple doing something you might admire, instead of making your spouse do it for you how about you start doing it for your spouse instead? You will in turn receive back something similar because people love reciprocating. Presenting each other with gifts that don't signify any occasion except to show love and affection would certainly be a good attention-grabbing action.

These gifts need not be expensive but simply thoughtful and sincere. One of the best gifts I got from Taurai was a bouquet of flowers he made for me on his day out at the hospice. Instead of thinking of himself and the pain he was in, he thought of me and wanted to make me happy.

Be Careful Of Actions and Behaviors

The actions and behavioral patterns expressed within a relationship, definitely illustrate in some way the kind of feelings evident from both parties, and this is usually a good sign of the strength of love and commitment.

Be careful in how your actions are interpreted if you're keen on keeping the relationship alive and strong. Self-awareness is very important in relationships.

I remember thinking that I didn't like shouting at Taurai because even after he apologized, I didn't feel great and it always took too long afterwards to get back my joy. I looked at ways I could express my displeasure about something without killing both our moods. Once I figured out how to do it, our connection grew deeper.

Be Cautious

There is a lot of research that has been carried out that clearly shows the actual level some actions and behaviors can affect a relationship; therefore, you should ideally think deeply before you act out because there are some things you can never undo. The idea of think before you act is recommended in relationships because a lot of drama can be a turn off for some people. One of my friends advised me to break up with Tau to see what he would do to win me back.

Being young and very naïve I went on to write a letter telling him that our relationship was over. I still remember his reply even today because it woke me up, *"Melody you know how much I love you and I know you love me too. I'm not into playing games with my heart so just this once I will let it pass but if you do this again then I will not be begging you to come back to me."*

I realized that playing with his heart wasn't fair if I didn't mean it, so I apologized. The two of you should take the time to ensure that all actions and behaviors are carefully expressed as once these actions or behaviors are exercised, the negative impact that it can depict will almost always be hard to justify or erase.

In some severe cases, such actions and behaviors may even cause destruction within the relationship and eventually end the relationship.

This is especially true when such displays are done in a very public manner for other people to witness. The embarrassment felt, would not be justifiable enough for the receiving party to forgive or forget. But this is a symptom of a bigger problem because by the time arguments get to public spaces they would have been festering and doing harm in private spaces.

I have to warn you to avoid bringing your family or friends into your arguments or fights. This is very dangerous because it can overcomplicate the situation. What usually happens is when we tell our friends about the issue, we exaggerate it to make ourselves look good.

You might not be aware this is what you're doing but we all do it by making him/her look like the villain in the story. If you then decide to forgive each other because you were overreacting, usually friends neverget the memo that the issue is resolved. Remember we all like to share bad news and not the good things because we don't want to be labelled as boastful or showoffs.

Even when they know that the issue has been sorted, they can start to have resentments towards your spouse. This is normal because they love you and want to protect you. They might even lose respect, which can be difficult because you need as much support as possible as a couple.

Sometimes you might divulge something so awful that you would be embarrassed to forgive them and rekindle the relationship. If you need help, get it from coaches, therapists, counsellors and other neutral parties.

We have been encouraged by the media and sitcoms to look at men as buffoons who really have no clue about life. We laugh at their lack of knowledge about ordinary things.

The problem with that approach is that it causes men to

be defensive and thus not trust women with their emotions. The gap between men and women keeps growing. Women are much more sensitive to actions and behaviors that depict them in a poor light, thus making such displays almost unacceptable for them. Women like to be appreciated and cherished and they won't accept it when they are being made to look bad in front of other people.

Being able to behave well and show some level of maturity and consideration is usually what most people would want extended to them, and in doing so all parties will be able to comfortably respect each other's boundaries of tolerance.

Hurt not healed will turn to rage. Be careful what you say and do because you will pay for it. Resentments always grow and become impenetrable walls. You cannot grow intimacy when one of you is hurting. One of my mentors, Alison Armstrong says, *"The only way you're going to get 100% participation in a relationship is if you're not bringing injuries to the table."*

Men too don't respond well to being publicly corrected or talked "down" to, so their partners should learn the vital lesson of keeping such actions and behaviors if absolutely necessary to the confines of their own private space. I used to talk about Taurai's tardiness at dinner parties with our friends. We would laugh and to me it was harmless until one day we were having friends coming over and he told me he wished they were not coming at all.

When I asked him why, he said because he was going to be the brunt of the jokes and to him it was humiliating. It made him feel less of a man. I was grateful he told me, and I never laughed at him with other people again because I never wanted him to feel less of the man he was.

Pay attention to some of the things you do and say in public about your spouse, as you might be unaware of how much damage you're causing to your relationship. When you wake up to doing something hurtful towards your spouse, apologise and stop doing it.

Ask for feedback from your spouse about some of the things you might be saying or doing that might be hurtful. He will appreciate your effort to be better.

Understand What the Problems Are

In any kind of relationship, the most common reason why problems or conflicts arise is due to misunderstandings.

This is something inevitable, given the fact that people live in an imperfect world.

If you are currently facing problems in a relationship, don't lose hope because you can still solve it.

Always remember that a locksmith never manufactures a lock without a key.

Understanding Problems

The most common mistake people in a relationship make is that instead of facing the problem, they try to escape it. Well, a problem is a problem and wherever you go, it will chase after you. So, the wisest way to deal with it is to face it.

A romantic relationship, specifically a husband and wife relationship, is very complicated. Failure to understand and figure out the root cause of the problem will surely lead to breakup or divorce. Thus, it is important for at least one, but if possible, both partners in the relationship to know how the relationship is supposed to work. This understanding will provide the relationship with long-term success.

The Difference between the Sexes

The major key to understanding the relationship dynamic is to know the differences between the sexes. Of course, there is a huge difference in the physical aspect, but what counts the most are the mental and emotional aspects between men and women. One of the main differences that both partners face in the relationship is the way they solve problems. Typically, they approach resolution from different angles.

When women are faced with a certain problem, they open it up to other people at great length. They will visit their girlfriends and discuss the conflict and solicit input and pieces of advice.

The main reason as to why women are fond of talking at

length about all the problems, they face in the relationship is that this is the way they solve them. For men, this is something very difficult to understand because they think that women like to get down to the heart of the matter concentrating on the problem. What they do not understand is that women are just examining the angles and their perception about every angle, with expectations that an ideal solution will appear.

On the contrary, men prefer to keep the problem to themselves and think deeply how they are going to find a resolution to it.

When they have figured out what they think is the best solution, they will begin to discuss the real problem with their friends, along with their solution to it. This scenario only implies that the difference between a man and a woman when it comes to solving problems can be a great obstacle.

The man might get fed up of the woman talking on and on about her problem, not knowing that this is her own way of figuring out a solution.

On the other hand, the woman may think that the man is insensitive and uncaring just because he does not talk about it. The truth is, he is thinking about it constantly, but he is not prepared to discuss it until he has already determined the right solution. This approach used to frustrate me a lot when Taurai went into his mental "cave". I thought he wasn't sharing with me because he didn't trust me or love me enough. Can you see how looking at it this way, can create problems?

Another great difference in understanding the relationship is that sometimes, women discuss matters they do not want help with or advice about. They just want to get the burden off their chest. For men, this is a strange concept. Most men have a purpose in talking about something. Basically, when men open up about a certain problem, it is for the intention of solving it.

Men really don't understand why women want to keep talking about something without doing or saying anything in order to solve it.

In a relationship, this plays out this way: the man will listen to whatever the woman says, then instantly propose a resolution to her problem. If the woman decides not to take his advice or solution then he will feel disrespected thinking, *"why did ask me if you didn't want my advice."*

He would think that he has done his part as a partner. However, to his surprise, the woman says that he does not listen and understand her feelings.

This is only an example and does not really apply in every situation, but it is true most of the time. Women want to talk about it out loud while men want to keep silent.

The next time you want to respond naturally during a discussion about a certain problem, just listen and try to understand your partner. Get curious and ask questions in order to get clarity instead of giving your opinion.

In doing so, you will be able to avoid fights and any unnecessary misunderstandings.

Honesty in Relationships

Honesty is always one of the most highly valued foundations within any relationship and this is very much demanded within a romantic relationship. For some reason, I have always wanted to be very clear and authentic in my relationship. I was so clear that I wanted to be me so that if being me wasn't enough then he can be free to continue searching for his true love.

This approach ensured Taurai was always honest with me even if it was to say, *"I am working on something right now that is stressing me out. Will you just listen while I talk it out?"*

In most cases, women are more likely to hold the element of honesty as a highly prized value when comparing to other human value systems.

In circumstances where women feel betrayed by men, honesty becomes even more valuable to them. In my experience, I have found that the more honest I am about how I feel and what I need to feel loved, the more honest my man was with me.

Even though women value honesty, they usually don't reveal what they need because they don't want to be a burden or seem too demanding. They believe if they are low maintenance then the man would choose them for marriage. This is not true at all. The most admired quality is not low maintenance but self-confidence.

Not telling your man what you need is dishonest. Not expressing what you need will confuse a man, as he won't know what to provide for you. Just because you haven't voiced something doesn't mean your spouse doesn't sense your disharmony. Knowing that we're all energy beings, your spouse will sense the disharmony and they will speculate about what might be going on. Knowing that we always assume the worst about things, can you see how dangerous it can be to withhold expressing what you need?

It is kinder to tell him, and if he is willing to give you what you need then he's a keeper. If he's not, then he's not right for you anyway.

The Importance of Honesty

In order to establish a strong and loving relationship the two of you need to be open and share your inner most hopes and dreams and you should be alert to the feelings and needs of the each other including your sex needs and fantasies.

Practicing being totally honest and kind as well as being alert to how your spouse is feeling can be pivotal to the growth and success of your relationship. It will make him see you as unique and different from other women he dated before.

Another very helpful feature to add would be to anticipate the needs of the other and work towards having these needs met adequately.

This will certainly be highly appreciated by the receiving party and will more than likely be reciprocated.

Some men need time to transition from work to home so they go straight into a private space for half an hour. Instead of resenting that give him what he needs so that he can give you the best of himself once he's ready. I have since learnt that some women need that transition time as well so give yourself the time if you need it and let your partner know of your needs too. If you have been working using your masculine energy, then it is helpful to reconnect with your feminine energy when you get home especially if you're in a relationship with a masculine man. This will help you to complement each other instead of becoming competitors.

You will find that when you need time off or just space to breath, he will be very happy to give it to you.

I could write a whole book just telling you about some of the things Taurai did for me because I was happy to give him the space to relax. I would also sit still so that he could just look at me (something he really loved doing and I didn't understand) and now I know he got fed from my energy.

I was happy to do it anyway even though I didn't understand why and sometimes it made me feel self-conscious. If you are really committed to making the relationship work, then taking the extra effort to pay attention to all the minor details within the relationship as a whole will give him and you good intel for creating opportunities to surprise each other.

It will help you to always be prepared for the unexpected and extend support that would be genuinely caring and considerate. Taurai had very bad eyesight so buffets were very difficult for him to navigate. I'm not sure when I started doing it, but I would ask him to choose our table and I would look at what was on offer.

By the time he was seated I would come back and tell him what was on offer. He would tell me what he wanted, and I would just fill a plate for him. I did it because I knew he was self-conscious about his eyesight and I wanted him to relax and enjoy the experience.

Taurai did so many things for me so that I wouldn't have to do them including getting up to get me socks when my feet were too cold, so I was happy to find opportunities to do loving actions for him too.

Most relationships eventually make the mistake of taking

each other's feelings and actions for granted, thus eventually becoming rather lazy and inattentive to the needs of the other party.

The best way to avoid that is to practice gratitude every day. After nearly divorcing, we just started to appreciate each other more and every night we would say, *"thank you for choosing me today, thank you for loving me and thank you for being my friend."* We said this to each other daily and this brought to the fore that we were both making a daily choice to be together.

Taking each other for granted of course is a rather negative and destructive mindset to develop as it will definitely be one of the reasons that contribute to the eventual downfall of the relationship.

Most of us are not aware how to grow relationships. We are skilled at how to start them all the romance stories we read or watch in movies never show you what happens after they kiss or say yes, I will marry you. Credits come up and that's the end. Like everything else in life if it doesn't grow it dies which means if you care about your relationship you need to tend to it. I can teach you how to grow your relationship from one stage to the other with ease and you might even enjoy yourself along the way.

If you practice honesty very early on in the relationship, both of you will be able to speak your mind without the limitation of deceit taking root in any area.

Mom taught me, one of the best lessons when I was a teenager. She said, "If a man buys you a meat pie and you don't particularly like meat pies, say thank you very much for the meat pie but I don't really like meat pies if you don't like them. Don't say, 'thank you thank you I love this', jump up and down and give him a kiss. If you do that every time, he wants to please you, he will buy you, a meat pie and you will probably get annoyed over time. It will make him feel unappreciated". Just in case you haven't figured it out yet, be open all the time and show him things that you genuinely love and appreciate then he will know how to get you the things you're going to love.

While everyone appreciates honesty in all circumstances, it is advised to be honest in a gentle and considerate manner, especially when feelings are involved. I practice mindfulness and kindness when dealing with people and being present. I find that I am kinder when I am mindful and present in my dealings with people.

Quality Time Together

Life today is busy and with Social media and television, etc. everyone's attention span apparently lasts nano seconds. Despite all this, human beings still need to feel connected with each other and the best and only way is to spend quality time with each other. This is true with all your relationships.

Commitments and distractions will often cause people to go through life without actually making an effort to be together, until the relationship suffers significantly enough to be on the verge of collapse.

Sometimes trying to resuscitate a dying relationship is more difficult than just taking the time to maintain it before resentments have grown too big.

You need to schedule quality time with each other no matter what. If you have, children make a plan to use your friends or neighbors to babysit for you so you get even one hour alone together per week.

Every day you are changing inside and outside and as you or

your spouse change if you don't experience that growth together you will wake up strangers one day.

Define what quality time means for each of you and make sure you give each other what each one needs. In this high-tech world sometimes people schedule going out, but they spend time on their phones and not with each other.

Make a pact to leave your phones in bags or pockets and just focus on each other. I remember there was a time when Taurai was in the middle of his PhD, I was working full time and was studying for a Masters' degree while we had a small child at home.

The only time we had together was when we went grocery shopping. We talked, laughed, told each other plans and challenges that had been coming our way.
Grocery shopping stopped being a boring chore to be something we both looked forward to. Do what you need to do if the relationship is important to you.

If you don't water plants and feed them, they will die,

and spending quality time together is like watering and feeding your relationship. This is true for all the relationships that you have. My dad used to take time to spend with us individually. He would ask one of us to walk with him to town or to the market, on the way he would ask about our dreams, challenges, and if there's anything he could do to help us achieve our dreams.

He would do that while holding our hand most of the time, which was very embarrassing. We all didn't like the experience at the time because we felt like we were being put under the spotlight but later when we had grown up and understood what had been going on, we really valued those times we got to really talk to him because he also shared his dreams for himself and stories of his life.

As my dad taught me, if you have children it is important for each of you to spend individual time with each child. Relationships are always different with 1 to 1 interaction time.

Some Insight

Making this effort and ensuring it is well noted and received is a good way to build a relationship that lasts through thick and thin. Some people might enjoy just sitting on the couch watching TV while others want to go out and do things.

You must take turns to do what the other wants to do in order to ensure both of you feel valued in the relationship. Spending quality time is something that needs planned attention and certainly concerted effort from both of you especially when there are significant work and family commitments to deal with, on a daily basis.

Without this effort, the relationship will eventually become stale and boring, which could lead to either of you seeking the missing link outside of the relationship. This could lead to emotional or sexual cheating.

When you start to look for what you need from outside the relationship, you need to understand that this could cause irreparable damage to the relationship.

Having said that I don't believe couples need to be all things to each other. Having friends and confidants outside the relationship is good to grow your capacity to love and benefits both of you with a support network. You need to be careful that the people you choose will not cause problems of trust in the relationship too. Supporting your spouse's other relationships can be very beneficial to your relationship from my experience. For some, establishing time for both parties to set aside may be a struggle but the insistence of this very healthy endeavor, will eventually bring forth good and beneficial results to the relationship.

The western culture of self-reliance makes it difficult sometimes to enjoy the benefits of life and community. If you happen to have young kids and find it difficult to spend quality time together start growing friendships with your neighbors and the elderly and involve them after a time getting to know them in minding your kids for short periods.

This will enrich your kids' lives; the people will benefit

from company and friendship that we all need, and you will have someone you can trust to mind your kids. It's a win win win. I know you might think you're too busy to start relationships with your neighbours but if you invest this time, you will be amazed at how beneficial it will be in your life.

Persistence in spending quality time with each other will bring rewards that will serve you in times of stress and struggle, as it will clearly show each of you the level of commitment; you're willing to take to strengthen the relationship.

If you find a partner unwilling to spend any time with you, then maybe they don't care about having a relationship with you.

This is also okay and should not be taken personally because trying to make someone be with you will stand in your way of actually finding the right person for you. It's like trying to swim upstream which is energy sapping and frustrating. Talking to each other about the importance of spending quality time is also very important, as this too will show your significant other, how serious both of you are committed to the improvement of the relationship.

'Date Night'

Date nights are special evenings and must be about romance, friendship, fun, excitement, entertainment, relaxation and growing closer together. In short, it must be free of any worries.

It is also important to plan the date night ahead of time because it will make you and your husband feel loved and honored. Do not leave strategizing until 5pm on the date night and if you are busy this week try not to, reschedule the date to the following week. Plan it in such a way that you look forward to it all week, which will add excitement during the week. Having something to look forward to will fill you up with happy hormones.

Date Night Tips

- Be Kids Again - The best way to enjoy your time together is to be kids again. Why don't you get tickets to the local aquarium or zoo? If you love playing board games and cards, then that would be a perfect way for you to enjoy your date night.

- Leave the technology out of it. No phones, iPads or any tech. That's enough said about that.

- Interview Your Partner - If you or your spouse has been super busy at work in the past few weeks, you can interview each other to discover new things. To make the interview more fun, draft unusual questions and do it over appetizers and cocktails.

It is very important to ask probing questions and take down notes. You can use your spouse's answers when buying him/her a gift that will make him/her surprised and happy. This is by far one of the best date night ideas that will surely fill your night with laughter.

Make it sexy - one of the areas that suffer because of the business of life is your sex life. Dress up, for those that do, shave your legs, make an effort and do it to entice and impress. You could stay home but have candles, sexy appetisers and music that turns you on. Be playful and flirty. Pretend you're just getting to know each other. Making love should not be left to whether you feel like it or not or worse as a reward for good behaviour but rather as a way to provide love, intimacy, connection and pleasure for both of you.

A date night is the perfect moment for you to rediscover each other. This will surely spur a romantic spirit in the place where you intend to hold the date. The only topics you shouldn't discuss on date night are the children and work.

If you have not yet tried to bond with your spouse due to your busy schedule at work, then now is the perfect time to start. By scheduling a date night once, a week, your relationship will be healthier and stronger as the years go by.

This is the secret to a happy married life. So, why don't you start planning now?

As well as weekly date night, organize quarterly long weekends or if you can manage it go away for a week. Use the week to relax, get massages or give each other massages, explore and expand your intimacy, plan how you want your relationship to grow. What is your vision for you personally and for you as a couple? This experience will make you feel rejuvenated and more connected.

Remember Why You Fell In Love

Challenges can either make or break your relationship. If you feel like there is no point in holding on, you had better think twice. Don't make any decision when you are angry because you will surely regret it in the end. I once heard Dr Phil say, *"You should walk away from your marriage only after doing everything you can to save it."* This is only true if you're not in an emotionally, psychologically and physically abusive relationship. There was a good reason why you decided to marry each other. What was it?

If you both can't seem to deal with your relationship anymore, why don't you spend time far away from each other for a while? You don't have to move out of your home, but you can go into introspective mode. Think about what is important and what is not important. This way, you will be able to realize your mistakes and know if you still want your partner in your life. Doing this even when you decide to separate will help you to clean the negative energy that you allowed to grow in your relationship. Not clearing it means you will take it to another relationship which ensure that relationship will face the same issues as well.

Travel Back In Time

The first way to know if your relationship is still worth saving is through remembering the first time you saw your partner and when you fell in love with him. By travelling back in time, there is a great tendency for you to rekindle the love you feel for each other. You will also be able to remember the happy and sad times you have shared and how you were able to get through them.

Apart from that, you should also figure out why you fell in love with your partner. Actually, this will give you a reason if you still want to hold on and try once again. Did you fall in love with him/her because of his/her positive attributes, which you think you can never find in anyone anymore?

Did he/she stand up for you at all costs even though

his/her life or reputation would be at stake? Did you fall in love with him/her because he/she made you a better person and made you realize that you are special? Did he/she make you feel happier?

Upon figuring out the answers to these questions, your heart will tell you what the next course of action is.

However, don't forget to use your mind because it will reprimand your heart the moment it goes out of control.

It is important to remember that we fall in love with people with qualities that we need to develop inside ourselves. This also means at some point those qualities will irritate us because they require us to change and grow.

Your brain will resist change as a way of protecting you but if you're aware that the irritation is just your brain doing its job, you will be able to get what you need and grow to be the best version of you. All your relationships give you what you need if you allow them.

Understand You Can Only Change Yourself

Did you know that the relationship itself is not the problem, but the people who are in the relationship?

This is the reason why you have to figure out what's wrong in you and change it. This way, you will be able to save your relationship that is on the verge of falling down.

Changing Yourself

Changing yourself is a self-help process. Thus, it is something which others can't do for you. It is a choice or decision and a lot of hard work.

However, this is not something that you can do over night; it requires time, patience and temperance.

To achieve this, you need to come to terms with yourself and admit your mistakes. To put it simply, you need to forget about your pride by sending it to hell.

Changing yourself is such a difficult process, as you have to think a hundred times before you make any moves.

You will feel like you are confined in a cage because you are afraid that you might make the same mistakes again.

Mind you, this should not be the case. Just like other processes, changing yourself is something that must be done one-step at a time.

Don't force yourself because it could lead to self-destruction. In your attempt to change yourself, you can also ask for help from the people who love you such as your friends, family or partner. Though they can't change you, they can help you. Love moves in mysterious ways, as they say.

In addition, don't forget that the only one who can heal your heart is the one who made it. If you ask for your heart to heal, it will get healed. You have a choice and if you make a decision, The Universe will support you in your decision. What paralyses a lot of people is that they get stuck in their situation and continue to go through it over and over instead of looking for something else that feels better. Freud called this, *"repetition compulsion"*, so the trick is to find something good to repeat.

Learn How to Be Considerate

Nobody's perfect and all people make mistakes. Remember human beings are selfish and look to see how they can benefit from a situation. Choosing to focus on your relationship as an enhanced part of the two of you will help you take action that will grow your relationship. In a relationship, you are not always right, and your partner is not always wrong. Seeking to be right all the time is a guarantee that your relationship will be unsuccessful because the person who is wrong will become resentful.

Both of you are responsible in one way or another if any problem or conflict arises. So, why not be considerate of each other? This is a sign of being humble.

What It Means To Be Considerate

If you don't want your relationship to break into pieces or to turn into ashes sooner or later, you need to be understanding through being considerate. But what does it really mean to be considerate? Does this relate to being a martyr? For your information, being considerate means accepting excuses and learning to say, "it's okay", especially when your partner has made an unintentional mistake. On the other hand, being a martyr means allowing your partner to abuse you by intentionally making the same mistakes over and over again.

Is it clear now?

When your spouse makes a mistake, don't take it like he/she did it to annoy you. Take it like they took the action to the best of their ability because of what they know at that time. For example, Taurai once went out drinking with his friends. Taurai didn't drive, so he took his nephew with him who didn't drink. The nephew was just supposed to drop him off and come back home.

The nephew decided to stay and after a while, they decided to leave where he had told me they were going and go to a party in another neighbourhood. A fight ensued at this party and the nephew ended up being severely injured. Instead of me being upset with Tau for going to this party where there were people he didn't know, I consoled him because he was already beating himself up for going there. We all make decisions that may turn out badly sometimes, that comes with being human but it doesn't mean we have to be punished for it.

Why Do You have to be Considerate?

Now, the million-dollar question is, why do you have to be considerate? The answer to this question is simple—to save your relationship.

In order to ensure that it will stand the test of time, a relationship needs two people working hard together. By being considerate, you are not giving your partner a chance to make a mistake again but giving your relationship a second chance.

What is great about being considerate is that you will be able to earn the level of consideration you have given to your partner in due time the moment you need it. As mentioned before, human beings are selfish by nature. Therefore, somewhere in time, you will surely make a mistake. Being considerate is like banking goodwill into your relationship. The more goodwill you have, the easier it will be for you when you hit a rough patch. You usually reach a rough patch when one of you is having self- esteem issues or doubts about yourself

But wait. What if your partner cheated on you? Do you still have to be considerate? Well, this depends on the situation. Of course, you have to give him/her a chance to explain.

After that, the rest will be history. It's only you who can decide for yourself because you are the one in the relationship. Just make sure that any choice you make will not make you regret it or it will haunt you for the rest of your life.

I once watched a video by Dan Savage, where he explained three things people get wrong about love and relationships. One of the things he said that I tend to agree with is that we're more committed and loyal to monogamy than we are to the people we're married to. Obviously, this is also within reason. If a person made you feel loved, cherished and taken care of and then one day they slipped and hooked up with someone once, do you just ignore all the history, property, children and everything you meant to each other or do you value the person and the relationship you have shared more?

If 60% of marriages are ending in divorce and the main reason being that they cheated, maybe we should start discussing what is acceptable and not acceptable in terms of our expectations of each other. Maybe we shouldn't allow infidelity to always be an extinction level event.

Maybe the best thing is to look at how else to make your sex life more adventurous, more fun and more frequent. Sometimes people don't want to give their spouse what they need sexually and yet they get hurt and feel betrayed when their spouse finds another outlet for their needs. I realise this subject is huge but I just wanted to introduce the idea that just because a neuro surgeon messed up and killed a patient doesn't mean they shouldn't practice as a doctor anymore. Just because your spouse cheated doesn't mean they don't love you and never loved you. The question is, do they still treat you well even after this slip up? Maybe we should be more forgiving.

When Taurai cheated on me with someone who was very close to us and we both valued as a friend, I was hurt, and I was very angry. I took responsibility for my contribution, like allowing lines to be crossed and not doing something about it in time.

We both allowed boundaries to be crossed in the name of friendship. I had seen it coming but decided to ignore it. We openly talked about it afterwards and he apologised and took responsibility for his actions. He did not blame me for doing what he did which some people would do.

We got past it only because we decided to be very real about what was not working for us anymore in our relationship. One of the things we really talked about was what was important to us in the bedroom. We stopped making assumptions about what made the other one happy. We also got experimental, trying new things we had never done before. We got open about doing some things for the other even though he or I might not have been that way inclined. Our sex life transformed and became spiritual as well as physical which really delighted us.

It took me some time to forgive him, but I forgave them both. Once I felt able and forgave him, I felt it easier to forgive my friend as well because she did not make a commitment and a vow to me. Even though I forgave her, I never allowed her to be in my relationship so much that she knew what was going on like before but I forgave them both. I was letting go of the negative emotions I had towards them. I also forgave myself for my contribution to the problem. As I worked on loving myself and filling my own cup and not expecting my happiness to come from my husband, he became more and more committed to me and to our relationship.

For some cheating might come in because someone does not feel seen or heard in the relationship. They are looking for fun and maybe a bit of adventure. They might want to feel alive once more through those heightened emotions of doing something dangerous. Whatever the reason might be you need to know it and NOT take it personally. People don't cheat because of something that is lacking in you but rather because of something they need inside them.

Concluding Thoughts

Every living person needs love in their life and sharing that love makes our lives richer and more fulfilling.

However, most people are so caught up with their own everyday agendas; they often forget the importance of demonstrating love towards each other, especially within a marriage. Sometimes they wait and only do something nice in reciprocation to the other instead of initiating.

There is a problem when marriage becomes a battlefield of personal agendas and winning instead of partnership and cooperation.

Almost every married couple who has been together for a while can relate to feeling disconnected in their own marriage at some point.

It is very helpful if both of you understand the importance of lovingly demonstrating love to each other within the marriage as this will often be the single most effective tool to keep the marriage from adversity and stress.

The skill to demonstrate love through actions and words is something that is expected, certainly highly regarded, and valued as most couples would confirm. Demonstrating love speaks volumes into the life and wellbeing of the relationship as it is an ideal and a significant way to show each other's love and commitment, which will make your marriage work. Ignoring your spouse and not showing them any love is a sure way to create resentment and negativity in your relationship.

This creates unnecessary animosity that causes stress and fighting with each other. Human beings respond really well to acts of kindness and love, so there is no need to stop from such displays of lovingness simply because a couple is married or has been married for a long time.

In fact, the longer the couples are together, the more the acts of lovingness should be encouraged and displayed. I remember reading a review of Barack Obama's book by someone on Amazon and his complaint was that Barack gushed too much, about how much he loves Michelle his wife in the book. I have heard some people complain about it but those who benefit from the gushiness never complain and if it works for you keep doing it.

Those who criticize it will never experience the sweet intimacy this provides to both parties.

When acts of kindness, appreciation and love are shared on a regular basis it leaves no space for couples to find fault with each other and even when difficult situations must be dealt with there is enough good will and positive outcomes are ensured. Therefore, the importance of demonstrating love should never be underestimated.

If the ideas brought up in this book resonate with you and you would like to learn more about how I can help you find love or help you with your existing relationship or how you can take your marriage from mediocre to awesome then visit my website www.heartpassioninstitute.com

Your Next Steps

I truly hope you enjoyed this book and learnt from my own experiences and got value from what I shared with you.

Whether you're looking for love, looking to heal from past trauma or heartache or looking to rekindle an existing relationship – it all starts from within.

If you feel like your relationship is already impossible to fix because several things have already happened, or you have suffered heartache in the past and feel like you'll never love again, don't give up so easily.

Seeking help is one of the best things we can all do. Often times we try to do everything ourselves, but we don't have to. When we get stuck, we get frustrated or we have one of those bad days where all the chocolate and wine in the world won't make us feel better, it can be difficult to express our emotions to loved ones, friends or family.

This is because they are so close to us, or perhaps you don't want them knowing how you really feel, at least not yet.

This is where I come in...

I have a Master's degree in Information Science. I am a certified Law of Attraction coach and a Certified Relationship Coach. Although I haven't experienced every situation personally, I have worked successfully with many women who have had different experiences.

I took my marriage from the brink of divorce where I was feeling unhappy, sad, depressed and betrayed. I felt like everything was wrong and I thought the best way was to leave my husband and find someone else.

No one I knew was able to tell me that it was possible to fix it, but they all told me to tolerate it. *"This is marriage, it sucks"*, they said.

They also told me marriage is hard work, but no one could tell me what that hard work entailed. I wasn't willing to live a life where I dreaded going home at the end of my work day or seeing my husband. Deep down I knew that things could be better but I had no idea how.

I had lost myself...

As a librarian and researcher, I looked at books and research papers on what makes a relationship thrive. I found out that it was all me.

I had lost myself. I thought being a wife meant giving up myself and doing everything to please my husband.

As I slowly started self-care practices (joining a gym, going out with my friends, buying new clothes for myself and asking my husband to help me when I needed help) I became happier and less overwhelmed.

I got my self-confidence back. I became more playful and creative. I stopped reacting and started responding to situations. I got to welcome, love and understand my Feminine Elegance and used it in my relationships to compliment my own energy and my husband's masculine energy.

Our relationship started to shift into a better partnership...

We became friends again, who were more honest, vulnerable and loving towards each other. Everything including our sex life improved significantly.

Joy became an everyday occurrence that we shared with each other. We found ourselves after 11 years of marriage feeling excited to see each other at the end of the day. We had an opportunity to experience the redemptive love that allowed us to connect deeply that we really became one.

I still remember Taurai's last text to me, *"If I was with you every time I think about you, I would be with you all the time."* It resonated with me because that's exactly how I felt about him.

When my husband passed away and I struggled, again to find my identity, peace and myself I discovered these gems and gold nuggets that I now use to help women find love in their relationships.

I took my experience in healing from emotional trauma and heartbreak together with everything I did and learnt that helped me heal and packaged it into a program that helps women like you heal emotional scar tissue from experiences in your past. Once you heal, you can then move on to getting clear about the type man you want and the type of relationship you would enjoy.

What I did in 3 years you can do in 5 weeks...

I will help you prepare, a place in your heart to plant new seeds of love that will grow and thrive. This love will help you harvest unimaginable happiness that you can share with other people in your life.

And it all starts with us having a conversation, to see if I'm a good fit for you and if you're a good fit for me. Below you will find a link to my personal calendar where you can schedule a time to speak with me.

Before you do, there's one thing I wish to stress... everything we discuss will be 100% confidential and will never be shared or spoken to another person.

If this is something, you're interested in visit www.heartpassioninstitute.com or email me directly on melody@heartpassioninstitute.com I promise to do everything I can for you and I look forward to helping you.

Melody Chadamoyo

Quiz - Are You Ready For a Relationship?

Tick whichever answers best describe you and your current situation.

1. How do you feel about what you have to offer in a relationship?

○ a) I don't know what I feel about myself most of the time

○ b) I feel like I have some qualities but I need to work on others

○ c) I am clear about what's missing and want to work on self-improvement

○ d) I genuinely like myself and feel good about who I am and what I have to offer

2. Do you still feel angry and upset about how your ex treated you in the past?

○ a) Yes, definitely

○ b) I am not entirely sure

○ c) I still feel anger but I am willing to let it go

○ d) No, it's over and I'm okay with that

3. My relationship strengths are:

○ a) I go with the flow to make my spouse happy

○ b) I respect the other person's values but I can be flexible with

mine

○ c) I know my values

○ d) I know my values and my deal breakers

4. My relationship weaknesses are:

○ a) I don't trust anyone

○ b) Lose my sense of self

○ c) I have no weaknesses

○ d) I don't know, I wish my ex's would tell me

5. My primary goal when starting to date someone is to

○ a) Make my ex jealous

○ b) Get serious

○ c) See if they are the one

○ d) Meet new people and see what happens

6. What would stop you from investing time for a relationship right now?

○ a) Lack of time due to work commitments

○ b) Lack of time due to family commitments

○ c) Not enough interest

○ d) Not knowing the qualities I am looking for

7. How often do you try new things?

- ○ a) Never I love my life the way it is
- ○ b) Once a year
- ○ c) Once a month
- ○ d) Every few weeks

8. Do you feel pressured by family or friends to get into a relationship?

- ○ a) Yes, and it's suffocating
- ○ b) Yes, but it doesn't really affect me
- ○ c) Not really
- ○ d) I am determined to find the right person for me

9. Do you find it easy to seek help when you need it?

○ a) Never

○ b) I would rather not

○ c) Sometimes

○ d) All the time

10. Do you think there could be a conflict between your career and your relationship?

○ a) Yes, my career is very important to me

○ b) At times, yes.

○ c) I am willing to make space for something this important

○ d) It is important to share my life with someone to make my life more fulfilling

11. Do you still feel the pain from past hurts and experiences?

○ a) Sometimes I lie in bed thinking about it

○ b) Yes, but I am willing to let it go now

○ c) I have forgiven but haven't forgotten

○ d) I have healed and learnt from the experience

12. Are your thoughts full of reliving past relationships?

○ a) Yes, I can't figure out what I did wrong

○ b) Sometimes, those were the best years of my life

○ c) Sometimes and I am open to creating new memories

○ d) No, I like living in the present

13. When it comes to your relationship, do you spend most of your time visualizing how it will be in the future?

○ a) I can't imagine what my future could look like

○ b) Sometimes I am sure but I don't believe I can get it

○ c) Yes, I can see clearly what experiences I want to have

○ d) Yes and I am open to new possibilities I haven't yet imagined

Submit your answers directly to Melody on melody@heartpassioninstitute.com for detailed results and feedback.

Your information will never be shared with anyone, ever.

Bibliography

1. Gray, John. 2002. Men *are from Mars, women are from Venus*. Chicago: Harper Collins.

2. Hendrix, Harville. 2005. *Getting the love you want: a guide for couples*. New York: Simon & Schuster.

3. Armstrong, Alison. 2012. *Celebrating partnership*. Available at http://a.co/0VOVpoi. Downloaded 20: March 2019.

4. Aál Al-Din Rumi & Barks, C. (1997). *The essential Rumi*.

5. Jung, C. G. (1969). Phenomenology of the spirit in fairy tales (R. F. C. Hull, Trans.). In H. Read et al. (Series Eds.), **The collected works of C.G. Jung** (Vol. 9 pt. 1, 2nd. ed., pp. 207-254). Princeton, NJ: Princeton University Press. (Original work published 1948)

6. Jahnke, Walter. (1984). Hermann Hesse ; *Demian: an exquisite novel*. Paderborn: Schöningh

7. Matthew 7:1 Holy Bible. Authorized King James Version.

8. Romans 2:1 Holy Bible. Authorized King James Version.

9. Lee, Ilchi. 2011. *The call of Sedona: journey of the heart*, Sedona. Best Life Media.

10. Peale, Norman V. 1956. *The Power of Positive Thinking*. Englewood Cliffs, N.J: Prentice-Hall.

11. Brown, Brené. 2012. *Daring Greatly: How the Courage to Be Vulnerable Transforms the Way We Live, Love, Parent, and Lead*. New York: Gotham Books.

12. Williamson, Marianne. 2011. *A Return to Love : Reflections on the Principles of "a Course in Miracles,"* New York, Harper Collins.

13. Spenser, Edmund. 1595. *My love is life to ice and I to fire.* Available at: https://www.poetryfoundation.org/poems/50271/amoretti-xxx-my-love-is-like-to-ice-and-i-to-fire. (Accessed: 27 May 2019).

14. When is the right time to consider divorce? Dr Phil. 2016 Available at: https://www.youtube.com/watch?v=ZxcGBB68PP0. (Accessed: 27 May 2019).

Why Self-Love is the Key to True Love

Why Self-Love is the Key to True Love